LONDON TUBE 101

Other Books by Anglotopia

101 Budget Britain Travel Tips
101 London Travel Tips
Great Events in British History
Great Britons
Anglotopia's Guide to British Slang

By Jonathan Thomas

Adventures in Anglotopia
Anglophile Vignettes
Visions of Anglotopia

LONDON TUBE 101

By
Anglotopia

Anglotopia Press - An Imprint of Anglotopia LLC
www.anglotopia.press

Printed in the United States of America

1st Edition: Decembber 2022

Published by Anglotopia Press, an imprint of Anglotopia LLC. The Anglotopia Press Name and Logo is a trademark of Anglotopia LLC.

Print Book interior design by Jonathan Thomas, all fonts used with license.

ISBN: 978-1-955273-23-7

Table of Contents

HISTORY

TRIVIA

CULTURE

USING THE TUBE

HISTORY

EXIT

A BRIEF HISTORY OF THE LONDON

The world's first underground railway, the London Underground, was constructed as a response to the city's rapid growth during the 19th Century. Today, it is the 11th-busiest subway system on the planet, with 1.379 billion passengers using it from 2016-2017. Its tunnels stretch for 249 miles throughout London, often overlapping and giving passengers plenty of options for getting from one place to another. The history of the Underground, its tunnels, and the people connected to it is truly fascinating. We hope that as you partake of this article, you'll submerge yourself in the history and lore and discover more than you knew about the Tube.

The Industrial Revolution of the late 18th and early 19th saw a shift in Britain's population from the farms of the countryside to the factories of the cities. Being the capital, London saw one of the largest influxes of new citizens, with the population of Great London tripling from 1,011,157 to 3,094,391 between 1801 and 1861. The increase in population also led to an increase in the amount of road traffic as residents of Outer London travelled to Inner London for work and back home each day. At the same time, the nation's seven major railways met in London, bringing in, even more, people and upwards of 200,000 people were crossing into the City of London each day.

The solution proposed was railways that would run steam trains underground to help move the city's new residents. By the 1850s, the groundwork had been set to create the system that the city would require. The first steam-powered railway trains were running across the country by the 1830s, linking Britain in an unprecedented manner. From 1825 to 1843, Isambard Kingdom Brunel and Thomas Cochrane had developed the tunneling technology that built the Thames Tunnel, enabling transportation of goods and people under the river and further linking the two sides of the city. Around this time, City Solicitor Charles Pearson had begun to argue for an underground transportation system and supported several schemes to have one built, including one in 1846 that included a central railway station that would be used by multiple railways. However, in that same year, the Royal Commission denied his plan.

Pearson pushed for his underground railway again in 1852 and, this time, found limited success with the creation of the City Terminus Company, which ran a rail line between Farrington and King's Cross. Unfortunately, while the scheme had the support of the city, the railway companies weren't interested, and it wouldn't be until the creation of the North Metropolitan Railway. The Bayswater, Paddington, and Holborn Bridge Railway Company was the impetus behind the Met's creation, which connected the Great Western Railway at King's Cross to the City Terminus Company's rail line, which the railway company had acquired. The company's attempts to get a bill through Parliament were often met with resistance until Royal Assent was given finally in 1854, by which point the company changed its name to the Metropolitan Railway, and its plans extended to include the London and North Western Railway as well as the Great Northern Railway.

Despite the difficulty in getting the funds raised due to the ongoing Crimean War, the Metropolitan Railway first opened in 1863, transporting 38,000 people on its first day and borrowing trains from other railways to assist. The first year saw a total of

9.5 million passengers, a number that increased to 12 million in the following year. This success meant that many new companies petitioned Parliament for new underground railways, and the District Railway soon followed. The two networks together would eventually form the basis of the Circle Line as well as parts of the Piccadilly Line and the District Line. The rivalry between the two railways' owners, James Forbes and Edward Watkin meant that the process of linking the two took twenty years and the lines continued to experience problems until the railways were amalgamated in 1933.

Over the next few decades, other lines would form from the various railway companies, including the Hammersmith & City Line (formed out of the Metropolitan Railway), the Northern Railway (formed by the City and South London Railway as well as Charing Cross, Euston, and Hampstead Railway), and the Waterloo & City Line (established by the London and South Western Railway). At the same time, steam engines started to give way to electric railways, though some steam engines would continue to see use even into the 1960s. The Underground Electric Railways Company of London, founded by American transport magnate Charles Tyson Yerkes, was established in 1902 and provided power to many of the electric railways. Digging technology also advanced to permit even deeper tunnels than that sub-surface lines that were first built.

THE YERKES ERA

The Metropolitan and District Railway lines were essentially created by digging trenches and putting a roof over them, so the first legitimately underground was the Northern Railway, which opened in 1890. This line ran from Stockwell to King William Street and later expanded Moorgate, Euston, and Clapham Common. Meanwhile, CCE & HR established the Hampstead Tube, and by the late 1920s, the two integrated into what we know as the Northern Line. Meanwhile, the Waterloo & City Railway opened in 1898 and named after its two stations. Two years later, the Central London Railway opened, running a line from Shepherd's Bush to Bank. The Baker Street and Waterloo

Railway opened in 1906 as one of the subsidiaries of the UERL and became known by its more popular name of "Bakerloo." In the same year, the UERL formed the Great Northern, Piccadilly, & Brompton Line that ran from Finsbury Park to Hammersmith.

A couple of major changes took place shortly afterward. The first, led by UERL publicity officer Frank Pick, was a clear brand for the company's lines. Borrowing from the London General Omnibus Company, Pick developed the roundel symbol for the UERL that would become synonymous with the Underground. He also introduced common signage and advertising throughout the lines that would become the basis for all other underground railways in the city. It wouldn't be twenty-five years between the creation of Pick's branding scheme that order would come to the chaos of London's fractured subterranean transport system when the London Passenger Transport Board was established in 1933. The Board effectively merged the city's transportation networks, including the underground railways, into a single entity that became London Transport.

Another major change for the Underground occurred two years prior, in 1931, when former UERL employee Harry Beck would produce his first design of the Underground map that would become the standard layout. Before Beck's map, diagrams of the underground railways tended to be geographical in nature and looked like a plate of brightly-colored spaghetti rather than an easily-understood interface. By "straightening the lines, experimenting with diagonals and evening out the distance between stations," Beck created a map that was simple and elegant, better understood by consumers than previous models. Beck attempted to sell it to the UERL in 1932, but the company wasn't interested. When he tried again in 1933, the UERL bought it off of him for £10 (or roughly £600) today. When the firm became part of London Transport, the map went with it and was altered several times over the decades, but Beck's initial design remained the basis for every subsequent version.

Beyond transport, the Underground found another use during the early 1940s when it became a key part of the city's war efforts. While people had taken shelter in the Underground's tunnels during the first bombing raids of World War I, there was an increased use of the disused tunnels as air raid shelters from 1940 to 1945. Additionally, the government made use of the Underground tunnels to store national treasures and as administrative offices for themselves and for the military. Some Tube stations even became small factories churning out munitions and airplane parts for the war. In many ways, the Underground network became its own small city during World War II.

Following the war, Clement Atlee's Labour government came to power, and a wave of nationalizing industries caught London Transport in its wake, incorporating the body into the British Transport Commission in 1948. The BTC ignored some of the maintenance needs of the aging Underground system but began construction on two new lines: the Victoria Line and the Jubilee Line. As the city had stopped growing due to the Green Belt that engulfed it, the two new lines would be focused more on alleviating current congestion rather than extending the network to new destinations. The Victoria Line opened in 1968, and the Jubilee followed in 1979, the latter named after Queen Elizabeth's Silver Jubilee in 1977. Beginning in 1969, the iconic phrase "Mind the Gap" could be heard over the stations' PA systems. The automated message was devised after it became too difficult for station staff and train drivers to verbally remind the passengers themselves, choosing a short phrase to save on costs. Sound engineer Peter Lodge recorded the phrase himself (as well as "Stand clear of the doors") after the original actor hired wanted royalties for his work. Other actors were later recorded saying the phrase, including Emilia Clarke, Phil Sayer, and Oswald Laurence, whose voice had been used since 1969 and was restored to Embankment Station at the request of his widow so that she could continue to hear his voice.

Eventually, the administration of London Transport was turned over to the Greater London Council, which instituted a system of fair zones in 1981 to help lower the rates on its buses and underground trains. In the ensuing years, London Transport introduced the Travelcard and the Capitalcard. 1984 saw the Underground become part of London Regional Transport under the Secretary of Transport, which would be a prelude to Prime Minister Margaret Thatcher's government dismantling the Greater London Council in 1986 and moving many of its responsibilities to the government or borough councils. The 80s also saw one of the worst disasters in the Underground's history when a fire started on one of King's Cross station's wooden escalators as the result of a still-lit match. The fire led to the deaths of thirty-one people, and the subsequent report led to new safety regulations.

Moving onto the 1990s, many of the trains received a fresh coat of paint after it proved difficult and costly to remove graffiti. In 1990, the Hammersmith & City line was crafted out the Metropolitan Line, which had been part of since the railway was created over a hundred years prior to this. Extensions continued in anticipation of the new millennium, and, at the same time, the return of a centralized London Government meant another change in administration for the Underground. Prime Minister Tony Blair's Labour government meant to create a new governmental organization for the city's boroughs and crafted the Greater London Authority, which took effect in 2000. At the same time, it created a new transportation body in Transport for London. TfL helped to create a public-private partnership in which TfL ran the trains while private companies helped to upgrade the lines.

Despite this, the government retained control of the Underground until 2003, when it returned to local control. The Oyster card was introduced that same year, along with busking in designated areas. As the decade went on, the Overground was introduced to relieve congestion along with new lines and stations, and the Overground has been credited as one of the causes of East London's revitalization. Crossrail then became the city's next great innovation, meant to further relieve congestion of the lines running between the home counties and through the city. In honor of the Queen's long reign, it was renamed the Elizabeth Line, a name that went into use in 2022 along with a purple roundel rather than the usual red. Recently, the London Underground moved to being open twenty-four hours per day on the weekends on select lines, mirroring the practices of other major world cities.

The first and one of the largest metro subway systems in the world, the London Underground continues to have a major role in the city. It is part of London's history, and its changes continue to reflect the change in the metropolis itself. The next time you find yourself on one of the Underground's trains, reflect on everything the system has been through over 150+ years and how you travel the same path as millions.

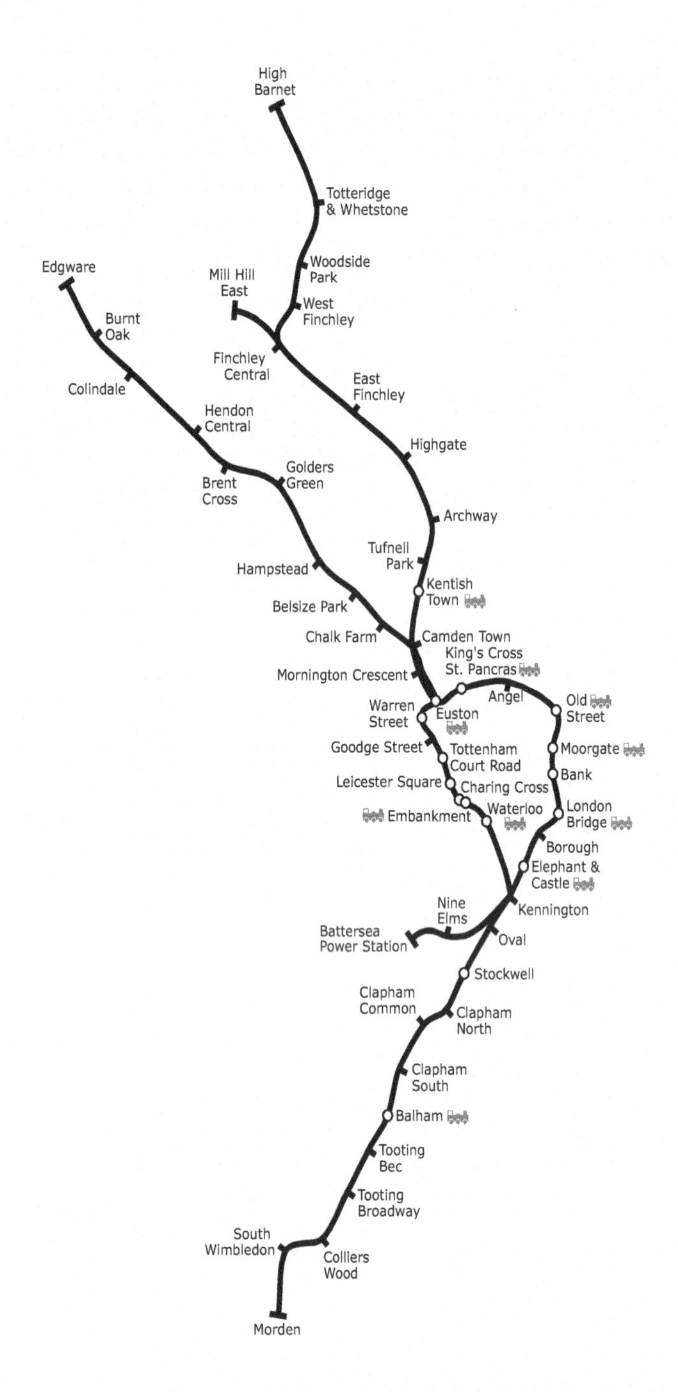

High Barnet
Totteridge & Whetstone
Woodside Park
West Finchley
Mill Hill East
Finchley Central
Edgware
Burnt Oak
Colindale
Hendon Central
East Finchley
Highgate
Brent Cross
Golders Green
Archway
Tufnell Park
Hampstead
Kentish Town
Belsize Park
Chalk Farm
Camden Town
King's Cross St. Pancras
Mornington Crescent
Angel
Old Street
Warren Street
Euston
Goodge Street
Tottenham Court Road
Moorgate
Bank
Leicester Square
Charing Cross
Embankment
Waterloo
London Bridge
Borough
Elephant & Castle
Kennington
Nine Elms
Battersea Power Station
Oval
Stockwell
Clapham Common
Clapham North
Clapham South
Balham
Tooting Bec
Tooting Broadway
South Wimbledon
Colliers Wood
Morden

A BRIEF HISTORY OF THE NORTHERN LINE

Looking at the London Underground map, you might be forgiven for thinking there's been a mistake and that you're looking at two separate lines instead of one. This is because the Northern Line has its origins in two separate railways that eventually merged into one even though they run on two parallel routes. However, it might be a good thing that the Northern Line is two halves of a whole since it's one of the busiest commuter routes in the city. Enjoy delving into the complex history of the Northern Line with us and you might learn some interesting things you never knew.

Going back to its earliest days, the Northern Line began with the City and South London Railway as well as the Charing Cross, Euston, and Hampstead Railway. C&SLR first opened in 1890 and CCE&HR began running in 1907. The C&SLR had the distinction of being London's first electric railway and its popularity meant that other Underground lines were quickly converted before the London Passenger Transport Board took over in 1933. Despite its popularity, however, low ticket prices and constant extension construction kept its parent company in a precarious financial condition. By comparison, the CCE&HR (also sometimes called the "Hampstead Tube") was not as popular and similarly suffered from financial difficulties.

By 1913, the Underground Electric Railways Company of London (UERL) took control of both lines but kept them as separate corporate entities. The two were joined together in the 1920s in a series of works that linked them at several stations at Euston Station and Camden Town. Such a joining had been planned much sooner but was delayed by World War I, with construction starting in 1922 and finishing in 1924. By 1926, new stations opened at Kennington and Waterloo, with the latter also providing a connection to the Bakerloo Line. Now linked together, further extensions were made to Edgeware and Morden.

After the London Passenger Transport Board took public ownership of all the underground railways and transformed them into the London Underground, it renamed the combined route as the Northern Line starting in 1937. The name came from the Northern Heights extension, which was never completed but helped to simplify things for the LPTB and passengers alike. Prior to that, it had a mismatch of different names including the Edgeware, Highgate, and Morden Line in 1933 and then the Edgeware-Morden line only a year later. Needless to say, the simplification of the name was certainly a welcome change.

Further extensions were made in the late 1930s, with the East Finchley station being the last in July 1939 before World War II put any future projects on hold. Little work was done until the 1960s and 1970s and even then, the projects were not terribly ambitious. It wouldn't be until 1988 and the reconstruction of Angel Station that the Northern Line saw any major construction projects. The redevelopment of the station would take about five years and not open until 1993. Beyond that, another extension of the Northern Line did not take place until the extension from Kennington to Nine Elms and the former Battersea Power Station opened in September 2021.

However, despite this, no further extensions north or south have been made, but it certainly doesn't seem as if they're needed. Despite its complicated origins and merger, the Northern Line hasn't experienced very many major incidents over its long history. At a length of 36 miles, the Northern Line sees roughly 206,734,000 passengers per year. In fact, for a simple two-hour period from 5 PM to 7 PM, 225,000 passengers each day. Thus, this unassuming conjoined route holds onto the crown of being one of the busiest lines in the London Underground.

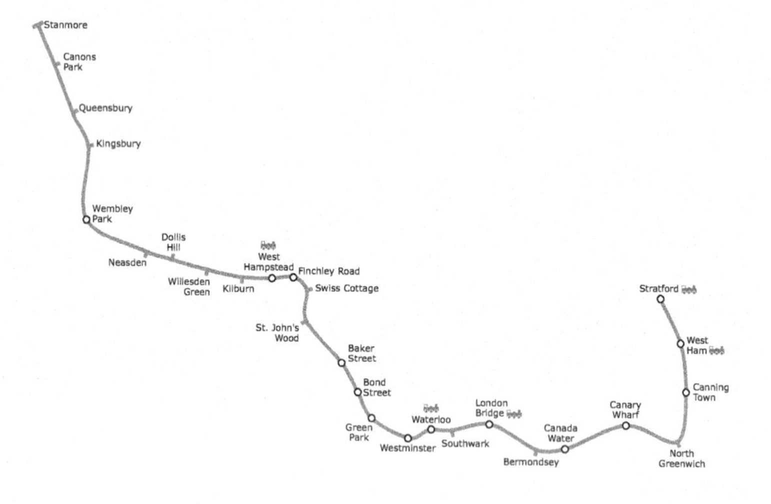
Stanmore
Canons Park
Queensbury
Kingsbury
Wembley Park
Neasden
Dollis Hill
Willesden Green
Kilburn
West Hampstead
Finchley Road
Swiss Cottage
St. John's Wood
Baker Street
Bond Street
Green Park
Westminster
Waterloo
Southwark
London Bridge
Bermondsey
Canada Water
Canary Wharf
North Greenwich
Canning Town
West Ham
Stratford

A BRIEF HISTORY OF THE JUBILEE LINE

Growing out of the London Underground's first line, the Metropolitan Railway, the Jubilee Line is named after Queen Elizabeth II's Silver Jubilee. Of course, this route for the Tube is much older than that, with origins that date back to the 1930s. Today it is one of the leading Tube lines when it comes to technology, and it has a fascinating history both before and after it received its official name. Join us as we explore the first London Underground line named explicitly after Her Majesty from its earliest days to the present.

The history of the Jubilee line begins in 1932 when the Metropolitan Railway opened a branch that ran between Stanmore and Wembley Park. The purpose for the new branch was to alleviate some of the commuter traffic coming out of the ever-growing London suburbs. This line proved more popular than originally predicted, and by the end of the decade, the line was absolutely packed on a regular basis. This problem was only made worse with a post-war flight of residents from the City of London to West London. To alleviate the problem, the Metropolitan Railway proposed a new line that ran along the existing railway from Edgeware Road to somewhere near Wilsden Green.

However, the London Passenger Transport Board had other ideas and moved the Stanmore branch to the Bakerloo line and closed the Lords, Marlborough Road, and Swiss Cottage, only opening them for special occasions or peak times. The new Bakerloo extension then opened in 1939, and the alleviation of increased post-war traffic was taken on by the Victoria Line which was completed in 1968. Even before the Victoria Line became operational, however, there was talk as early as 1965 of another line that would be referred to as the Fleet Line.

Construction on this new Fleet Line got its start in 1971, though funding questions and the uncertainty of the line's final destination meant it would be constructed in phases. The first phase would run from Baker Street into Central London with stops at Bond Street and Green Park before terminating in a new station at Charing Cross. Phase 2 would extend along the River Fleet to Fenchurch Street, then Phase 3 would go under the river to Surrey Docks (known today as Surrey Quays on the DLR), and Phase 4 would continue on mainline suburban tracks to Addiscombe or Hayes.

Tunneling took place from 1972 to 1979, and during this time, the line's name was changed to Jubilee to celebrate Queen Elizabeth's Silver Jubilee in 1977. Prince Charles opened the line on April 30, 1979, and service began on May 1. Despite the initial plans for the phased extensions, no additional stations or rails were added to the Jubilee Line until the 1990s. By that point, the development of the London Docklands had taken center stage, and the Jubilee Line was instead extended from Green Park to Stratford, foregoing the Charing Cross station and passing through the Docklands before heading north after passing through North Greenwich.

Since these expansions, the Jubilee Line has ever sought to be at the forefront of new technology for the London Underground. It received a seventh car on each of its trains beginning in 2005, and in 2011 it converted to Automatic Train Operation, increasing service capacity and decreasing wait times. Beginning in March 2020, a leaky feeder was installed that could provide the line with 4G service for commuters, a feature that is to be expanded to other Underground lines in the future. If you want to have a ride on the Jubilee Line, keep an eye on the London Underground map for the silver/gray path and hop on for an experience you won't forget.

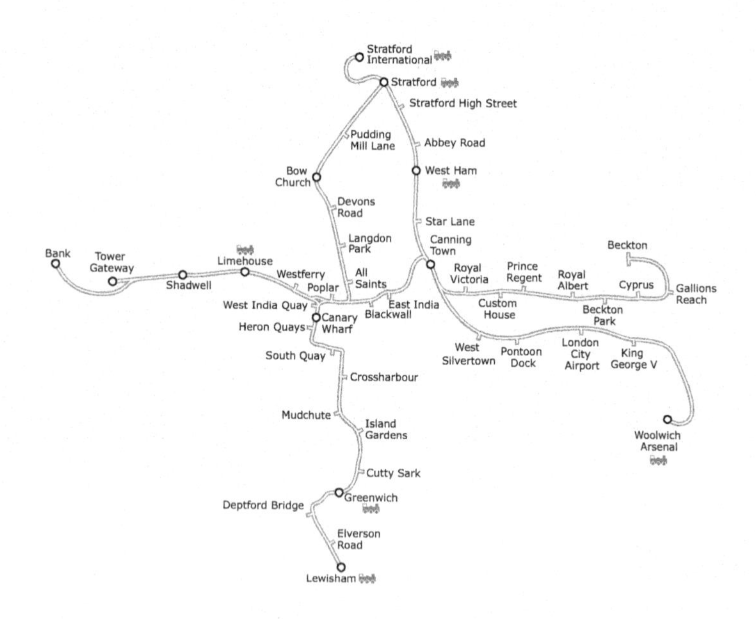
Stratford International
Stratford
Stratford High Street
Pudding Mill Lane
Abbey Road
Bow Church
West Ham
Devons Road
Star Lane
Langdon Park
Canning Town
Bank
Tower Gateway
Limehouse
Shadwell
Westferry
Poplar
All Saints
Royal Victoria
Prince Regent
Royal Albert
Cyprus
Beckton
Gallions Reach
West India Quay
East India
Blackwall
Custom House
Beckton Park
Canary Wharf
Heron Quays
South Quay
West Silvertown
Pontoon Dock
London City Airport
King George V
Crossharbour
Mudchute
Island Gardens
Woolwich Arsenal
Cutty Sark
Greenwich
Deptford Bridge
Elverson Road
Lewisham

A BRIEF HISTORY OF DOCKLANDS LIGHT

Moving onto an oft-forgot member of the London Underground, the Docklands Light Railway is a unique entity of all the lines. The DLR is also one of the youngest parts of the Underground, as it's only been around since 1987. As it celebrates its 35th year of ferrying Londoners around the Docklands, we're going to explore its history from its origins through multiple extensions that have brought DLR's route to about 24 miles. Read on, and you might find there is plenty of interesting history related to DLR that you'd never considered.

The Docklands Light Railway came about as part of the redevelopment of the Docklands by the London Docklands Development Corporation. After World War II, the area around the Docklands became less utilized for shipping due to the development of containerization. The docks had been connected to the national railway system through the London and Blackwell Railway, but that closed in 1966 due to a lack of traffic. When the LDDC got its start, a light railways system was envisioned as part of the development, helping to solve issues of transporting Londoners from Central London into the eastern part of the city.

The LDDC then commissioned London Transport to explore several different routes, and the LDDC and London Transport had hoped to use existing routes to develop DLR, but it appeared that there was no capacity to integrate the light railways into the existing network. Two routes were developed from Stratford to Island Gardens and Tower Gateway to Island Gardens. The DLR was meant to be constructed as cheaply as possible, and only 11 trains were purchased, with only 9 or 10 expected to run at peak times. DLR was also developed to be entirely automated to cut down on staff, with the trains and stations both being automatic. However, this didn't mean that the trains had no human operators in case of problem, with Passenger Service Agents who not only patrolled the trains but could take control of them if necessary. While the Underground didn't have the capacity at the time to link to DLR, the railways also made use of existing lines wherever possible with little new construction required.

Queen Elizabeth II then opened the line in 1987 and was immediately much more successful than predicted. It wasn't long before the hourly ridership numbers were outpacing the original predicted daily figures. This necessitated an increased number of trains and soon extensions to DLR. The railways experienced numerous growth spurts throughout the 1990s and 2000s, expanding first into the City of London and the Royal Docks, then to Greenwich and Lewisham, and finally to the London City Airport and Woolwich. Eventually, the trains were further expanded to three cars while further expanding out to Stratford International rail station in anticipation of the 2012 Olympics. If you were to look at the DLR map as it exists today, you'd think it resembled a giant squid with its tentacles flailing about the Docklands.

Originally run by London Regional Transport, the LDDC took over around 1992 and was then operated by private sector franchisees from 1997 to the present. When Transport for London came about in 2000, they took over the management of DLR while continuing to run it through franchises, with the current franchisee being KeolisAmey Docklands LLC, who has held the franchise since 2014 on a seven-year contract that was extended another four years in 2021 to run until 2025. It remains to be seen how DLR will continue to grow further in the future, though Transport for London will certainly be up to the challenge.

WAIT HERE FOR
FIRST CLASS

A BRIEF HISTORY OF THE CIRCLE LINE

Prior to its expansion with a line to Hammersmith, the Circle Line lived up to its name by forming a loop that encircles much of inner London. Running through Chelsea and Kensington, the City of London, Hackney, Islington, the City of Westminster, and now to Hammersmith and Fulham, the Circle Line runs through practically every major Underground and railway station in London. This, of course, shouldn't be surprising since it was born out of two of the London Underground's original lines. Punch your Oyster card and join us on a journey down the tunnels of the Circle Line's history from its earliest days to the present.

As mentioned, the Circle Line actually got its start from two of London's oldest Tube lines: the Metropolitan Line and the District Line. Then known as the Metropolitan Railway and the District Railway, both lines were in their earliest days when a Parliament select committee recommended an "inner circle" of railway lines that connected the city's railroad termini. The two separate lines ultimately had a falling out and the prospect of uniting them into a circle wasn't realized until Parliament intervened in 1884. Each company ran services in a separate direction, with the Metropolitan trains ran "outer rail", or clockwise, services and the District ran "inner rail", or anti-clockwise, services.

In 1882, the Metropolitan extended services to a temporary station at Tower Hill that was replaced with a permanent station in 1884. This completed the inner circle and afterward, the Metropolitan Railway began to run all outer rail services by 1908. Meanwhile, the District Railways was running into financial problems and needed to refinance around 1901. It used to opportunity to fully electrify its services and amalgamated with the Underground Electric Railways of London. This caused some issues between the Metropolitan and District railways that were using different electrical systems, a problem that was solved when the Metropolitan converted its stock to be compatible with District's system.

In 1933, both the Metropolitan and District railways were absorbed into the public London Passenger Transport Board, forming part of the London Underground. The shared loop between the two lines became formally known as the Circle Line in 1936. On the Underground Map, the Circle Line appeared in the same shade of green as other sub-surface lines including the Metropolitan Line, the District Line, and the Hammersmith & City Line. The Circle Line wouldn't become its own distinct line until 1948 when it was denoted by a black border and didn't receive its yellow color until 1949.

Between 1959 and 1960, Circle Line trains were increased up to six cars to match those of Hammersmith & City Lines. The Circle Line trains were also integrated with maintenance at the Hammersmith Depot. For decades, Circle Line stock had been hand-me-downs from other lines but finally received their own brand-new trains in 1970. Single-operator trains were proposed as early as 1972 but weren't actually introduced until 1984. The Circle Line was also yet another Underground line that was partially privatized in 2003 and run by Metronet until the company went into administration in 2007, at which point it reverted back fully to the management of Transport for London.

Moving further into the 21st Century, the Circle Line was

one of the Underground railways affected by the July 7, 2005, terrorist bombings when two explosive devices went off around 8:50 AM. The bombs killed 15 people, including the two suicide bombers, and the line remained closed until August 8. In 2009, the Circle Line extended to include the Hammersmith & City Line to Fulham, giving it a little branch off of Paddington, turning the circle pattern into a spiral. Most recently, the Circle Line was closed along with the Waterloo & City Line in March 2020 as part of a pandemic lockdown restricting all but non-essential travel. Now back open and ferrying passengers once again, it remains to be seen where the Circle Line will go in the future.

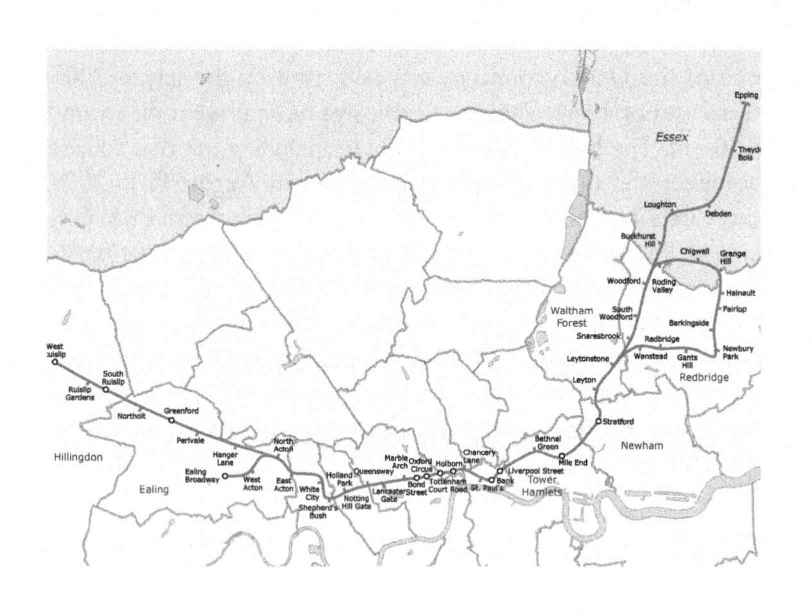
Epping
Essex
Loughton
Debden
Buckhurst Hill
Chigwell
Grange Hill
Woodford
Roding Valley
Hainault
Fairlop
Waltham Forest
South Woodford
Barkingside
Snaresbrook
Redbridge
Newbury Park
Leytonstone
Wanstead
Gants Hill
Leyton
Redbridge
South Ruislip
Ruislip Gardens
Northolt
Greenford
Stratford
Hillingdon
Perivale
Hanger Lane
Ealing Broadway
North Acton
West Acton
East Acton
Ealing
White City
Shepherd's Bush
Holland Park
Notting Hill Gate
Queensway
Lancaster Gate
Marble Arch
Oxford Circus
Bond Street
Tottenham Court Road
Holborn
Chancery Lane
St. Paul's
Bank
Liverpool Street
Bethnal Green
Mile End
Tower Hamlets
Newham

A BRIEF HISTORY OF THE CENTRAL LINE

For over 121 years, the Central Line has been a central part of the London Underground. Its importance is can be exemplified by the fact that it's the longest Tube line in the city at forty-six miles that serve forty-nine stations, from West Ruislip to Essex. The Central Line has been a vital part of London's history and culture since it opened in 1900, and we're going to take you on a journey through the Central Line's history from its origin to its terminus and all the important moments in-between that make it so significant.

The Central Line's origins start about eleven years before it actually opened. The Central London Railway established itself as a corporation in 1889 and published a pamphlet announcing its intention to present a bill to parliament for a new underground railway. Unlike previous underground railways that had started as steam-powered, the Central Line was proposed to be entirely electric. The original route proposal started on Queen's Road and ended at King William Street in the City of London with a connection to the City and South London Railway. The Metropolitan and District Railways to the north and south of the proposed line objected, along with the City of London Corporation, the Dean and Chapter of St. Paul's Cathedral, and Joseph Bazelgette (the designer of the city's sewer system).

With the original bill killed by the opposition, the CLR tried again in 1891. To address concerns, the route was modified, in the process making it longer with one end at Shepherd's Bush and the other at Cornhill. This bill was passed by Parliament and received Royal Assent in August, but a few months later, the CLR submitted another bill modifying the route again, this time reaching the Royal Exchange (now Bank Station) and turning upwards to end at Liverpool Street where it would connect with the Great Eastern Railway's terminus. This proposal received royal assent on June 28, 1892, and then the real work began—fundraising.

It took nearly three years for the CLR to raise the money it needed for construction and to hire the contractor, deciding upon the Electric Traction Company Limited in 1894. It financed the remainder of the railway by selling stocks and was finally ready to start construction in 1896. The CLR hired three engineers and used the tunneling shield method that had been utilized for the City and South London Railway. To alleviate concerns about the destruction of buildings, the tunnels followed the roads above, which is why the most central part of the line has such a windy path. Tunneling was completed in 1898, and additional delays caused by negotiations with the City of London nearly bankrupted the CLR and necessitated another bill in 1899 to extend the time for opening to another year. Meanwhile, many of the above-ground stations were designed and constructed by Hell Bell Measures. These were single-story structures with a beige terracotta edifice that could permit additional commercial or residential construction on top of them.

Finally, the Central London Railway opened on June 27, 1900, with the event attended by the Prince of Wales (the future King Edward VII). This was just a day before the 1899 bill was due to expire and the line didn't open to the public until July 30. With initial prices at two pence, the CLR quickly earned the nickname "The Twopenny Tube" from the Daily Mail, which was eventually shortened to "The Tube," a nickname now applied to all of the London Underground. Reversing loops were added in 1902, followed by further extensions of the line in 1907, 1909, and 1911. As competition amongst lines increased, the CLR opted to promote itself through technological advancements, but all the efforts to compete became fruitless when the lines were all incorporated into the London Passenger Transport Board in 1933.

The Central Line was largely unaffected by World War I, but World War II was a different story. Parts of the line were converted into underground aircraft munitions factories, while many stations served as bomb shelters during the Blitz. Further expansions were halted in June 1940 and resumed after the war ended, expanding to Greenford in 1947 and West Ruislip in 1948. Further expansion to the west was denied due to London's new Green Belt, but the line further advanced to the northeast all the way to Epping.

The history of the line in the late 20th and early 21st centuries was largely quiet, focused on modernizing the line in the 1990s. Sadly, tragedy struck in 2002 when a train derailment at Chancery Lane resulted in the deaths of thirty-two passengers. The line was also one of many that were partially privatized with Metronet that same yet but reverted back to Transport for London in 2007 when Metronet went into administration (bankruptcy). Since that time, the Central Line has remained in the public care and in public service, transporting over 280 million passengers per year.

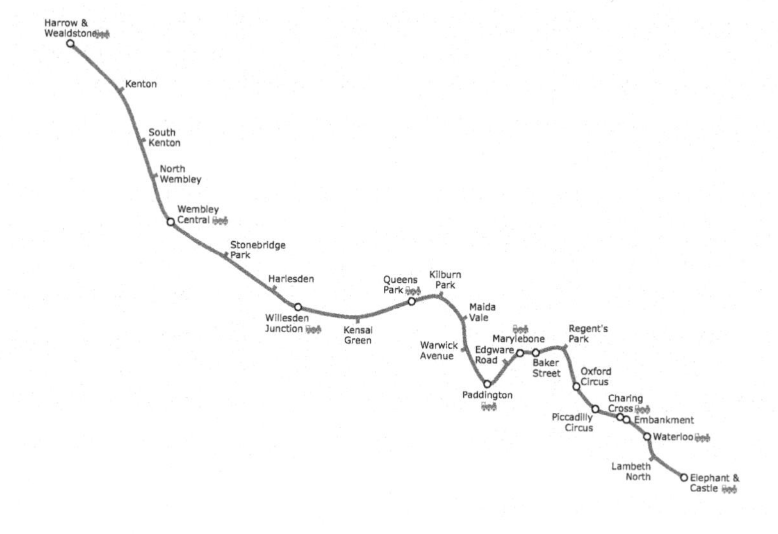
Harrow &
Wealdstone
Kenton
South
Kenton
North
Wembley
Wembley
Central
Stonebridge
Park
Harlesden
Willesden
Junction
Kensal
Green
Queens
Park
Kilburn
Park
Maida
Vale
Warwick
Avenue
Paddington
Edgware
Road
Marylebone
Baker
Street
Regent's
Park
Oxford
Circus
Piccadilly
Circus
Charing
Cross
Embankment
Waterloo
Lambeth
North
Elephant &
Castle

A BRIEF HISTORY OF THE BAKERLOO LINE

Like a lightning bolt running through the city, the Bakerloo line gets passengers where they're going nearly as fast and has been doing so for over 100 years. Its name is a portmanteau of two parts of London through which it ran when it first opened in 1906. You might be interested to learn, however, that its history goes back well before this and into the 19th Century when it was very nearly the first major rival to the Metropolitan Railway. Join us as we explore the history of one of the London Underground's Bakerloo Line from its earliest history to the present.

As mentioned, the roots of the Bakerloo line go back well before its opening in 1906. Two years after the Metropolitan Railway (now the Metropolitan Line) opened, a pneumatic railway was proposed called the Waterloo and Whitehall Railway. Trains would have used air pressure to provide power for the trains' propulsion. However, the line was hit by a financial crisis during 1866 while it was under construction, and the proposal was ultimately abandoned in 1870. Parliament incorporated the partly-constructed line in 1882. Another attempt was made at establishing a line in this same year, this one an electric railway called the Charing Cross and Waterloo Electric Railway. However, the Metropolitan Board of Works opposed the plan, and after the corporation's owner died in 1883, the plan fell apart.

After the success of the City and South London Railway electric line in 1890, a private bill was put forward to Parliament in 1891 proposing the Baker Street and Waterloo Railway. Three other similar bills were proposed in the next year, and a select committee was formed to decide which should be approved. The committee approved a plan that ran from Baker Street to Waterloo with stops at Oxford Circus, Piccadilly Circus, Trafalgar Square, and Embankment. In 1896, an extension to Marylebone was added to the plans. Raising funds proved to be one of the line's earliest challenges, especially after one of the financiers, Whitaker Wright, was convicted of fraud in 1904 and committed suicide after the verdict was read.

Construction began in 1898, and when the line first opened in 1906, a pamphlet published by the Underground Electric Railways Company of London suggested that it had been started by a group of businessmen who wanted to get from the city to the Lords Cricket Grounds. Nearly from the beginning, most Londoners shortened the railway's name to "Bakerloo." Stations were designed by Leslie Green with similar features, including steel frames, flat roofs, and oxblood-colored tiles. One prominent example still in use is the Oxford Circus station. By 1907, the line expanded to Edgware Road in the North and Elephant & Castle in the South. The line expanded several more times before it was consolidated with other underground railways by the London Passenger Transport Board in 1933.

To alleviate congestion on the Metropolitan Line in the 1930s, the LPTB transferred services for Stanmore to Bakerloo in 1939. The tunnels for the new Bakerloo services were built underneath the Metropolitan tunnels. Stanmore would stay with the Bakerloo line until it was transferred to the Jubilee Line about forty years later. No other major changes were made for years, and proposed extensions of Bakerloo further south didn't materialize until 2019, with an extension to Lewisham via Old Kent Road due to open in 2030. For now, however, the Bakerloo line runs from Elephant & Castle to Harrow & Wealdstone and will still get you to the Lord's Crick Grounds in a hurry if you really want to catch the match.

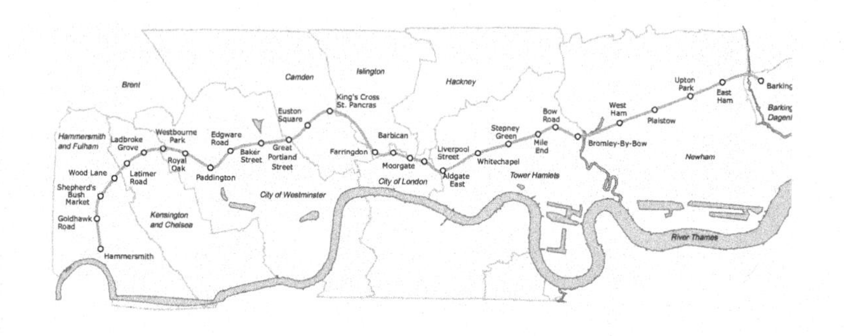
Brent
Camden
Islington
Hackney
Hammersmith and Fulham
Ladbroke Grove
Westbourne Park
Edgware Road
Euston Square
King's Cross St. Pancras
Wood Lane
Latimer Road
Royal Oak
Paddington
Baker Street
Great Portland Street
Shepherd's Bush Market
Goldhawk Road
Hammersmith
Kensington and Chelsea
City of Westminster
Barbican
Farringdon
Moorgate
City of London
Liverpool Street
Aldgate East
Whitechapel
Stepney Green
Mile End
Bow Road
Tower Hamlets
Bromley-By-Bow
West Ham
Plaistow
Upton Park
East Ham
Newham
River Thames

A BRIEF HISTORY OF THE HAMMERSMITH & CITY RAILWAY

Every day people take a London Underground train to get from point A to point B without considering the history of the lines they take. Underground Tube lines actually have some pretty fascinating histories, including the Hammersmith & City Line. This line actually started as an extension of the Metropolitan Line, which had opened in 1863 as the first underground railway in the world. At the time it opened the Metro ended at Paddington. Even before it opened, Parliament approved an extension that ran all the way to Hammersmith and was built off of the Great Western Railway's mainline. The Hammersmith & City Railway then opened on June 13, 1864.

In the early days of the railway, the line had two intermediate stations at Notting Hill and Shepherd's Bush. Train carriages would attach or detach at Notting Hill to switch over from the Met's gauge rail (4' 8.5") to the Great Western Railway's gauge (7', 0.25") to take the branch line down to Kensington. Starting in 1867, the Metropolitan Railway and Great Western Railway ran the line together, operating three running rails that utilized the gauges for both the Met and the GWR. Over the ensuing years, several other lines were connected to Hammersmith & City, and the line was extended out to Aldgate in 1876 and Whitechapel in 1884. Electrification for the line occurred in 1906, with services shortened to Whitechapel and the line to Richmond being withdrawn that year. Services to New Cross and New Cross Gate were then withdrawn in 1914 when the East London Railway was electrified.

The next big change for Hammersmith & City came in 1933 when it was amalgamated into the London passenger Transport Board with every other Underground railway in 1933, designated the Hammersmith & City Line but still part of the Metropolitan Line. They relieve congestion from Whitechapel, in 1936 the London Passenger Transport Board diverted trains from the East London Line to Barking, which remains the line's eastern terminus today. Service for the line during WWII was mostly uninterrupted except in 1940 when service to Kensington Olympia was temporarily suspended due to bomb damage. Between 1959 and 1960, the H&C and Circle Line railway vehicles were converted to the same formation, and their depot was located in Hammersmith. As part of the Metropolitan Line, Hammersmith & City ran goods as well as people up until the 1960s and 1970s. One-person operation was then introduced to the line in 1984.

A new chapter for Hammersmith & City began in 1990 when it was split off from the Metropolitan Line and officially designated the Hammersmith & City Line in its own right. The line's official color on the London Underground map is "Underground Pink Pantone 197". In 2003, the Hammersmith & City Line, much like the Metropolitan Line, was partially privatized and run by Metronet in a public-private partnership. This lasted until 2007, when Metronet went into administration and Transport for London resumed full management. From 2012 to 2014, the line's C69 and C77 trains were upgraded to S7 stock trains to increase their capacity. Today, the line is nearly 16 miles long, with a total of 29 stations running from Hammersmith to Barking. The entirety of the Hammersmith & City line is shared by numerous other Underground lines, and it is one of the few that doesn't have any portion of track or stations to itself.

And this brings us to the end of the history of the Hammersmith & City Line. While not as notable as other members of the London Underground, it shares a great deal of its history with the Metropolitan before striking out on its own to be one of the most-used Tube lines with 114 million passengers a year. Think about that the next time you set foot on a Hammersmith & City train.

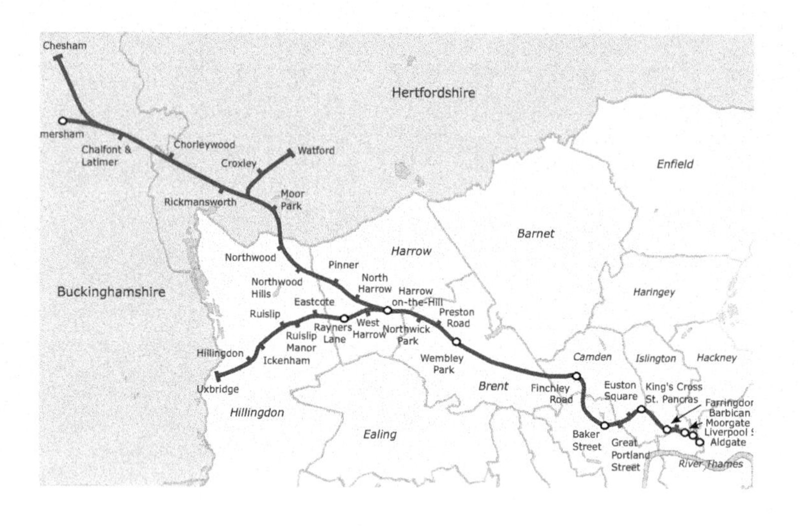
Chesham
Hertfordshire
mersham
Chalfont &
Latimer
Chorleywood
Watford
Croxley
Enfield
Rickmansworth
Moor
Park
Barnet
Harrow
Northwood
Pinner
Northwood
Hills
North
Harrow
Harrow
on-the-Hill
Buckinghamshire
Haringey
Eastcote
Preston
Road
Ruislip
Rayners
Lane
West
Harrow
Northwick
Park
Ruislip
Manor
Hillingdon
Ickenham
Wembley
Park
Camden
Islington
Hackney
Uxbridge
Brent
Finchley
Road
Euston
Square
King's Cross
St. Pancras
Hillingdon
Barbican
Moorgate
Ealing
Baker
Street
Great
Portland
Street
Aldgate
River Thames

A BRIEF HISTORY OF THE METROPOLITAN LINE

Of course, if we're going to start anywhere, why not start with the line that began it all? The Metropolitan Line has been around since its opening in 1863 and was the first underground transport railway anywhere in the world. This gives the Met the richest history of any public transport in London and on the planet. Join us as we take you on a journey through the history of the Metropolitan Line and kick off a fantastic new series on Londontopia.

The Metropolitan Line began as the Metropolitan Railway, a goods and services railway that went from the city's heart to the Middlesex suburbs. With the advent of the Industrial Revolution, more and more people flocked to London from the countryside looking for work, growing the city exponentially. This, of course, also led to a massive amount of traffic and the need for new railways that helped carry people into the city. As Parliament searched for a solution, Charles Pearson became the champion of an underground railway, succeeding in the passage of the North Metropolitan Railway Act in 1854.

The next several years were spent raising funds for the

railway's construction which began in 1860. Construction used the "cut and cover" method, where a shallow trench was dug and then covered over. During construction, several accidents befell the line, including a Greater Northern Railway train running off the uncompleted tracks in 1860; in 1861, the excavation in Euston collapsed the tunnel and caused damage to surrounding buildings, and in 1862 a sewer burst flooded excavations of the tunnel. Construction finished towards the Spring of 1862 after costing a total of £1.3 million. The first trip across the entire line then took place in May 1862.

The coming of the new year marked the opening of the Met to the public, and the new transportation line was an immediate success. The original line was only 3.75 miles and ran from Paddington to Farrington Road, but the success meant the line quickly expanded to St. Pancras and Moorgate Street. The Met's management didn't see themselves as a commuter railway originally but a major competitor for the more traditional railway lines. Only ten years after opening, the Metropolitan Line expanded out to Hammersmith, Kensington, and South Kensington. The lines continued to shift as new underground railways were introduced to the city and the London Underground came to be more of a travel service between the suburbs and the city.

The 20th Century saw a number of changes to the line, including the introduction of electricity in 1900, though this was halted during World War II, and steam locomotives ran on the Metropolitan until 1961. In 1933, the Met was consolidated with all the other Underground railways to form the London Passenger Transport Board, officially changing its name from Metropolitan Railway to the Metropolitan Line. This effectively shut the door on the Met becoming a major railway in its own right, and as Greater London expanded further through the next few decades, new fast-service lanes were added to reach even deeper into the London suburbs.

In 1988, the East London and Hammersmith & City Lines split off to form their own branches of the Tube. Some parts of the line were privatized into a public-private partnership with Metronet in 2003, but that only lasted four years until Metronet went into administration (a process similar to bankruptcy in the US) in 2007 and Transport for London took full control once again. Today the Metropolitan Line runs all the way from Aldgate to Chesham in Buckinghamshire. Approximately 54 million riders use it every year, proving that the oldest of the Underground's lines is still one of its most popular.

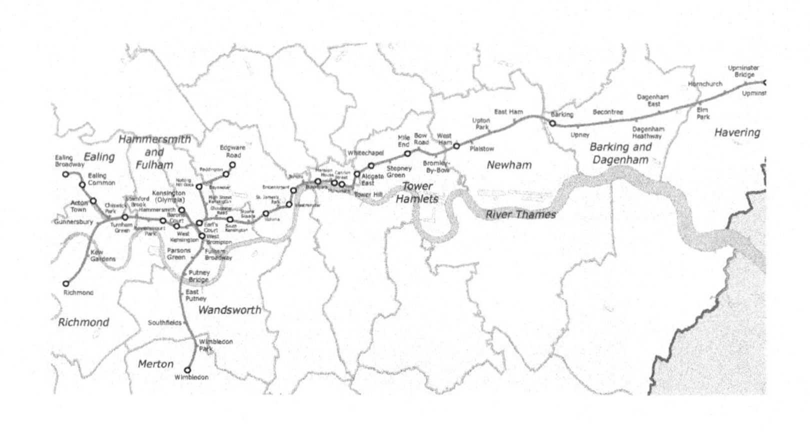
Ealing Broadway
Ealing
Ealing Common
Acton Town
Gunnersbury
Kew Gardens
Richmond
Richmond
Hammersmith and Fulham
Chiswick Park
Stamford Brook
Turnham Green
Kensington (Olympia)
Hammersmith
Barons Court
West Kensington
Earl's Court
West Brompton
Parsons Green
Fulham Broadway
Putney Bridge
East Putney
Wandsworth
Southfields
Wimbledon Park
Merton
Wimbledon
Edgware Road
South Kensington
St. James's Park
Whitechapel
Mansion House
Cannon Street
Aldgate East
Tower Hill
Stepney Green
Mile End
Bow Road
Bromley-By-Bow
West Ham
Plaistow
Tower Hamlets
Upton Park
East Ham
Newham
River Thames
Barking
Upney
Becontree
Dagenham Heathway
Dagenham East
Barking and Dagenham
Elm Park
Hornchurch
Upminster Bridge
Havering

A BRIEF HISTORY OF THE DISTRICT LINE

One of the oldest lines in the history of the London Underground, the District Line has a rich history that has been simultaneously full of competition and cooperation. From its earliest days as the District Railway to the formation of the Circle Line as well as electrification, municipalization, and branching out over greater London, the District Line has a fascinating history that we'd like to share with you. Grab your Oyster card and jump aboard as we take you all the way to the end of the line on a tour through the District Line's history.

The Metropolitan Railway's success after it opened in 1863 led to numerous bills petitioning Parliament to adopt other underground railway schemes throughout London. To help make decisions about which lines should be accepted, the House of Lords set up a select committee to go through the proposed bills. The select committee was persuaded by a proposal for a line south of the Metropolitan with the idea that they would eventually merge and link together many of the city's railroad termini. The Metropolitan Railway's chair and three of its board members, as well as the engineer for the railway, helped to establish the Metropolitan District Railway, but it was kept as a separate corporation to raise funds independently of the Met.

Work on the line began in 1864. Unlike the Metropolitan Line, which was purposely constructed under the city streets to prevent damage to buildings, the District Railway's construction did not follow a similar plan, and compensation was paid to the owners of buildings above its planned route. The line opened its first section in 1868 and utilized trains from the Metropolitan Railway. However, by 1870, the District Line was in debt and the decision was made to split it off from the Met. The next year the District Line began to operate with its own trains and the railway extended to West Brompton and Mansion House. The two railways still cooperated somewhat by providing a transport service between their two termini at Mansion House and Moorgate Street.

Competition then took over and the two lines didn't complete the circle as originally intended until 1884 with Parliament's support. Still suffering from financial woes, the District Line amalgamated with the Underground Electric Railways Company of London in 1901. It fully electrified its railway stock and electric services began running in 1903. Along with the other underground railways in London, the District Railway was municipalized in 1933 when it was brought under the management of the London Passenger Transport Board. From that point onward, it became known as the District Line.

The breakout of World War II suspended services intermittently and after the war, the District Line was nationalized along with the rest of the UK's and London's railway services, both over and below ground. The Acton Town to South Acton shuttle service was then discontinued in 1959. By the 1970s, the Hounslow Branch became the Heathrow Branch when it was extended all the way to the airport. Over time, the line extended all the way to Upminster in the east and branching out at Earl's Court with termini at Edgeware Road, Kensington, Ealing Broadway, Richmond, and Wimbledon. With its green color, on a map, it looks like a tree that's fallen over.

The District Line's history passed this point has very few major noteworthy incidents. D stock trains were introduced between 1979 and 1983, and then single driver trains became commonplace starting in 1985. The District Line fell under the operation of Transport for London in 2000 which was formed as part of the new Greater London Authority. Along with much of the Underground, the line became part of a public-private partnership in 2003 with Metronet that ended when Metronet went into administration in 2007. While the line's history has been relatively quiet ever since, it remains a vital part of transportation in the city, seeing some 208 million passengers per year.

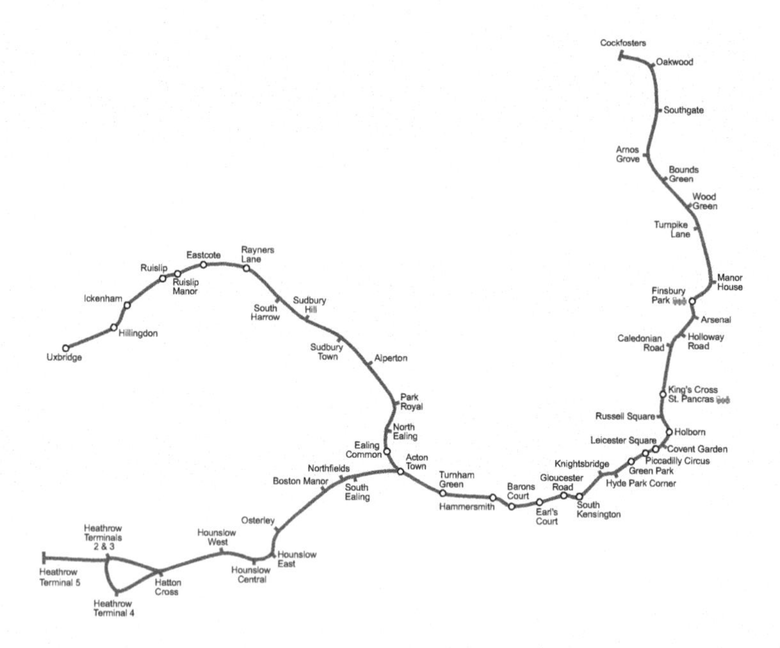
Cockfosters
Oakwood
Southgate
Arnos Grove
Bounds Green
Wood Green
Turnpike Lane
Manor House
Finsbury Park
Arsenal
Caledonian Road
Holloway Road
King's Cross St. Pancras
Russell Square
Holborn
Leicester Square
Covent Garden
Piccadilly Circus
Green Park
Hyde Park Corner
Knightsbridge
South Kensington
Gloucester Road
Earl's Court
Barons Court
Hammersmith
Turnham Green
Acton Town
Ealing Common
North Ealing
Park Royal
Alperton
Sudbury Town
Sudbury Hill
South Harrow
Rayners Lane
Eastcote
Ruislip Manor
Ruislip
Ickenham
Hillingdon
Uxbridge
South Ealing
Northfields
Boston Manor
Osterley
Hounslow East
Hounslow Central
Hounslow West
Hatton Cross
Heathrow Terminals 2 & 3
Heathrow Terminal 4
Heathrow Terminal 5

A BRIEF HISTORY OF THE PICCADILLY LINE

In our next entry on the history of the various Tube lines, we explore the history of the Piccadilly Line, which hits some important spots in London from Heathrow Airport to Buckingham Palace. As with many of the Underground's lines, the Piccadilly Line has its start in the old underground railways that preceded the creation of the London Passenger Transport Board and the London Underground as we know it. From its earliest days at the turn of the 20th century through to the 21st Century, we'll take you on a journey down the dark blue line of Piccadilly and share its fascinating history.

The Piccadilly Line got its start at the advent of the first electric underground railways in 1906 with the creation of the Great Northern, Piccadilly, and Brompton Railway. This railway itself was actually the merger of two railways that hadn't been built and were linked with another section between Piccadilly Circus and Holborn. An additional deep-level tube line was added between South Kensington and Earl's Court to finish the GNP&BR route, with the line first opening in December 1906. At the time, the ridership figures ended up being quite low as they were overtaken by the prior introduction of electric trams and busses.

Not too many years after the line opened, the GNP&BR found itself merged with other electric railways into the London Electric Railway Company in 1910. Also, that year, the line's station at Earl's Court had the first escalators installed on any underground line. In 1912, the line got its first extension when it went past Hammersmith to Richmond along the District Railway line. The act granting the extension received Royal Assent in 1913, but the outbreak of World War I caused the construction to be delayed until the 1930s. Around the same time, an extension north past the terminus at Finsbury Park was discussed, and the London Electric Railways Company was absorbed with other Underground lines by the London Passenger Transport Board.

It was with the formation of the London Underground that the railway transformed into the Piccadilly line, with its dark blue color denoting it on the map. A year before, the first extensions opened westward, resulting in the Piccadilly Line splitting into two lines that went to Hounslow West and Uxbridge. During World War II, at least a couple of stations were fitted with blast walls and converted into use by various governing boards. In the decades post-war, the line was further extended northwards to Cockfosters, and in the 1970s, a new extension was made all the way to Heathrow Airport.

The Piccadilly Line experienced its first major tragedy in 1987 when a fire began in the escalator shaft of the line's still-wooden escalators at King's Cross Station. Within minutes, flame and smoke billowed out into the ticket hall, resulting in injury or death to nearly everyone there. Thirty-one lives were lost that day, and shortly after, the escalators were rebuilt with metal to prevent another disaster. In 2005, the Piccadilly Line experienced another loss when a suicide bomber detonated on the train between King's Cross St Pancras and Russell Square as part of the 7/7 terrorist attacks. The attack on the line resulted in the largest number of casualties that day at twenty-six lives lost.

But in spite of these terrible events, the Piccadilly Line

celebrated its 100th anniversary in December 2006. A couple of years later, the Piccadilly Line welcomed an extension to Terminal 5 at Heathrow, making it easier for airline passengers to get off their flight and head straight to the heart of the city. Today the Piccadilly Line serves 210 million riders per year, making it the fourth-busiest line in the London Underground.

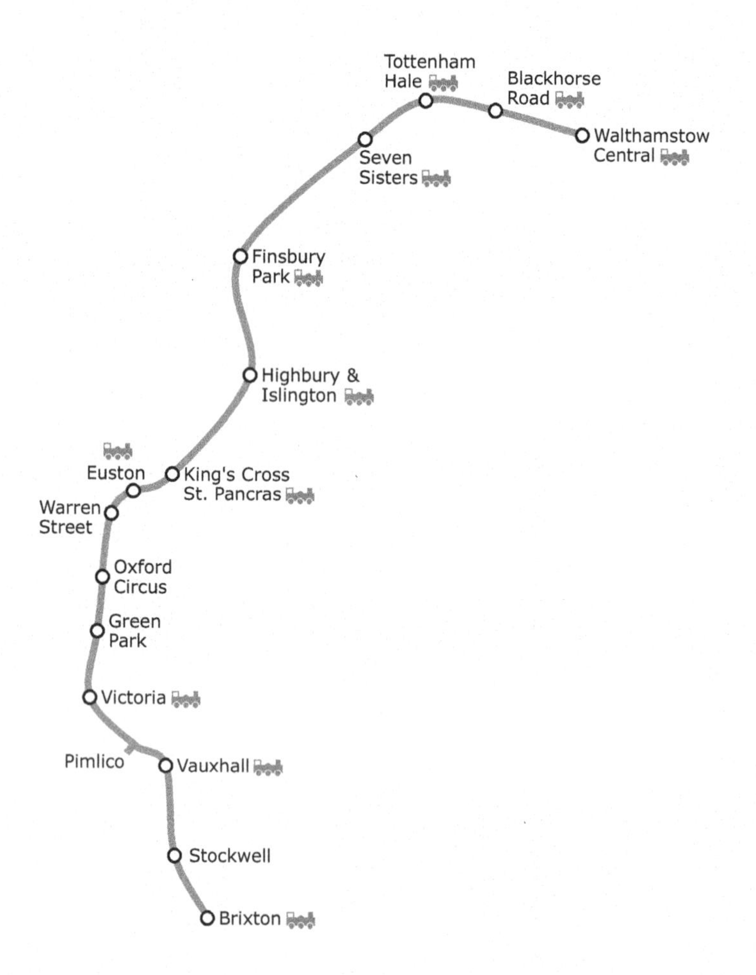
Tottenham
Hale
Blackhorse
Road
Walthamstow
Central
Seven
Sisters
Finsbury
Park
Highbury &
Islington
Euston
King's Cross
St. Pancras
Warren
Street
Oxford
Circus
Green
Park
Victoria
Pimlico
Vauxhall
Stockwell
Brixton

A BRIEF HISTORY OF THE VICTORIA LINE

It might be hard to believe, but the Underground line named after the United Kingdom's second-longest serving monarch, is actually one of the babies when it comes to the Tube. It's also one of the only Tube lines to have just one extension. Running from Brixton in South London to Walthamstow Central in the northeast of the city, the Victoria line first opened in 1968, but its history starts well before that. The first mention of the new line came in 1943 as part of the County of London Plan. Five years later, the British Transport Commission set up a working party that proposed a line running from Victoria to Walthamstow Central.

The line as proposed would help to alleviate congestion that had been a problem in Central London since the 1930s. The proposed line would also link several important railway stations including Victoria, Euston, King's Cross, and St. Pancras. To accomplish its goals, the BTC looked at the possibility of a deep-level tube and got a bill approved by Parliament in 1955. That same year, the line was christened the Victoria Line after several other names were suggested such as the Mayfair Line, the West End Line, Walvic (Walthamstow-Victoria), and the Viking (Victoria-King's Cross). Ultimately, British Transport Advertising decided on Victoria because it "sounded right".

Despite the approval from Parliament and the new name from British Transport Advertising, nothing began immediately due to funding issues. It wasn't until 1959 that the first test tunnel was constructed between Tottenham and Manor House underneath Seven Sisters Road. This test tunnel was eventually incorporated into the line. Construction on the rest of the Underground line then started in 1962 and continued until 1968. The Victoria Line opened on September 1, 1968, and the first train rain from Walthamstow Central to Highbury and Islington. Queen Elizabeth II then formally opened the line on March 7, 1969, when the rest of the line was completed all the way to Victoria.

The Victoria Line was revolutionary when it opened as it was the first automatic passenger railway in the world. All the driver had to do was close the doors and press a couple of buttons to send the train on its way to the next station. The train is operated by a central control room, sending coded impulses along the railway. Additionally, the initial design for the stations was in blue and grey tile, and the designers had some fun working puns into the decorations based on the station's name, such as a ton of bricks for Brixton.

Meanwhile, even before the Victoria Line came online, London Transport was already planning the line's first and only extension. The extension from Victoria to Brixton was intended to be a "park and ride", with commuters parking at Brixton Station and taking the Victoria Line further into the city since the station was located at the southern section of the motorway box. Construction began the same year that the Victoria Line opened and completed in 1971, with Princess Alexandra taking the first ride from Brixton to Vauxhall. Further extensions were considered but to date, have not progressed beyond the proposal stage.

Beyond the Brixton extension, not much more has changed in the ensuing years, with the exception of stock and facility upgrades. In 1991, a walking path was constructed to connect the Victoria Line with the Circle Line at Victoria Station. Platform bumps were added in 2010 and 2011 to increase accessibility by providing no-step access to the trains. Twenty-four-hour Night Tube service was then introduced in 2015. Today, while the Victoria Line is one of the newest and shortest of the London Underground railways, it remains an important part of transportation services in the city.

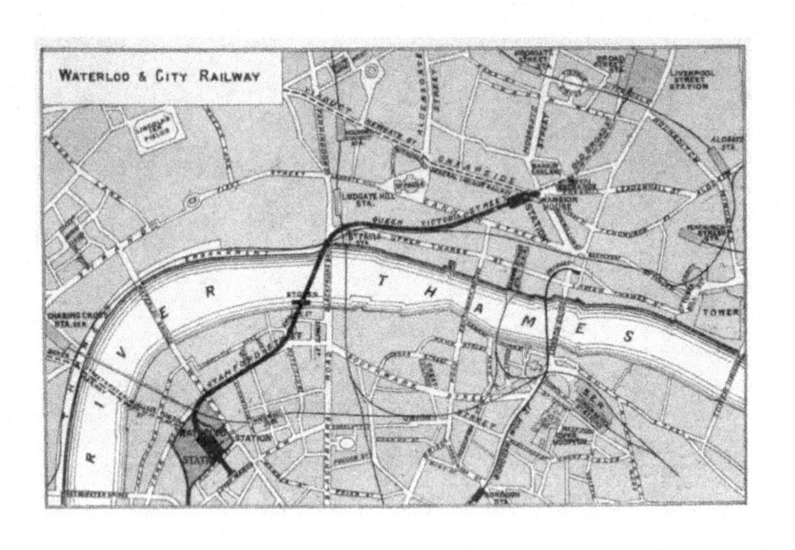
WATERLOO & CITY RAILWAY
LIVERPOOL STREET STATION
CHEAPSIDE
MANSION HOUSE
LUDGATE HILL STA.
QUEEN VICTORIA STREET
UPPER THAMES ST
R
T
H
A
M
E
S
R
I
V
E
R
STAMFORD ST
STATION
TOWER

A BRIEF HISTORY OF THE WATERLOO & CITY LINE

The Waterloo & City Line has the notorious distinction of being the shortest of the Underground lines in London. It's so short, in fact, that it only goes between two stations (Waterloo and Bank) with no stops. Its name, coupled with its status as a glorified shuttle train, has earned it the nickname "The Drain" since it flushes commuters down the Tube to one station or the other. The Waterloo & City Line can be found on the Underground map thanks to its turquoise color and is just under 1.5 miles long. You wouldn't think such a short railway would have much in the way of history, but that's where you would be wrong. Join us as we examine the long and short of the Waterloo & City Line's history.

The line's history begins in 1864 with the proposal of a pneumatic railway dubbed "The Waterloo and Whitehall Railway" that would run between Waterloo and Great Scotland Yard. Work began in 1865 with great enthusiasm, but the overall cost proved to be too much, and the project was ultimately abandoned by 1868. Thirteen years later, another project was promoted called the Waterloo and City Railway which would have been an overground line to Queen Street, but that project also floundered when the cost was projected to be £2.3 million. The third try was the charm, however, and the Waterloo & City Railway Bill was introduced in 1891 with financial backing from the London & South Western Railway at a cost of roughly £500,000.

Progress on the bill was slow-going, though, and the London County Council objected to the proposed railway, concerned that the Tube line would be too small and wanting instead a mainline terminus the size of Waterloo under Bank. Ultimately the bill received Royal Assent in 1893 and the construction of the Waterloo & City Line began the next year in 1804. Using a tunneling shield system, it took approximately four years to construction the railway line. A new station was constructed under the overground Waterloo Station with arches to support its upstairs neighbor while the opposite terminus was constructed in the heart of the city and known as City. The name of the station would later change to Bank around 1940.

Waterloo & City Line opened to passengers on August 8, 1898, and proved to be an almost immediate success with the business commuters who put the line at capacity at the beginning and end of the day (also referred to as "the rush"). It proved so popular that more cars were ordered in the next year and put into service in 1900. By 1906, the London & South Western Railway purchased the W&CL and began operating it. As the line was owned by one of the big railway companies, it was not absorbed into the London Underground in 1933 when the London Passenger Transport Board formed. The line continued to operate independently of the Underground until 1994, after which it was operated by the Central Line.

In the 21st Century, Waterloo & City Line experienced a refurbishment in 2006 when the Londoner Underground was partially managed by Metronet. While the train doesn't normally run on Sundays, this changed for the 2012 Olympics to help with the capacity increase during the games. In the late 2010s, Bank Station got its own upgrade that tied its entrance into Bloomberg's London headquarters. Come 2020, the COVID19 pandemic shut the line down for a total of fifteen months due to lockdowns and the decreased demand on the service. The Waterloo & City Line came back into operation in June 2021 and remains an integral commuter train for workers returning to their offices.

SWAN VEST

TERROR ON THE TUBE: A HISTORY OF DISASTERS ON THE TUBE

First off, we should point out that despite the horrific title of this article, the Tube is an incredibly safe mode of transportation when you're in London. However, no safety record is perfect, and the Tube has, on rare occasions, been the target of terror groups. In fact, the London Underground sees over one billion passengers per year and averages an accident per 300 million journeys, so the odds of anything happening are incredibly minute.

However, I'm not here to write about everything going well. In its long history, accidents and attacks go back as far as the Underground has existed. The first took place in 1883 set by Irish republican terrorists as part of the Fenian dynamite campaign. A planted bomb on one of the trains exploded near Paddington station, damaging not only that train but also a train passing by it and injuring sixty-two people. Two years later, another Fenian bomb struck on a train at what is now Euston station. The first accidents also took place in the same year as the first Fenian bomb attack, when two slow-moving trains collided at Farringdon Street station.

Another bombing would not occur until 1897 when the Aldersgate Street station (now Barbican) was hit by an explosive device left by an anarchist group. Sixty people were injured in the blast, but only one died as a result of his injuries. A bomb was discovered at the Westbourne Park station in 1913 but did not explode and was believed to have been planted by Suffragettes, though this was never proven conclusively. From that point until the Good Friday agreement, the only terrorist bombs were those planted by the Irish Republican Army, with the first attacks coming on February 3 as IRA terrorists left bombs in luggage at Tottenham Court Road and Leicester Square stations and on July 26 at King's Cross and Victoria Stations. Combined, the attacks only produced one fatality and a handful of injuries.

A different kind of bomb would strike as war came to London in 1940. During the German bombing campaign known as the Blitz, a 1400 kilo semi-armour-piercing bomb hit 32 feet underground and exploded just above the cross passage at Balham station. The bomb left a crater in the street above that a bus crashed into and damaged a water main that flooded the tunnels below and hampered rescue efforts for the people using Balham as a bomb shelter. None of the 600 people in the shelter were killed by the bomb or the collapse, but reports stated that some people may have drowned in the rising waters or in the panic that ensued as people attempted to escape, and estimates ranged from 64 to 68 fatalities.

Unfortunately, this would not be the last disaster that would take place during the war, though the next would not come as a result of German bombs. Bethnal Green station had also been requisitioned as an air-raid shelter, and it was here on March 3, 1943, that tragedy struck. As people made their way down the stairs to the station following an air raid siren, a woman and child tripped, causing other people to fall, and quickly creating a mess of entangled bodies that totaled 300. The resulting panic caused 173 deaths due to the shelterers on the bottom being crushed and/or asphyxiated. To this day, it remains the worst civilian loss of life in the Underground.

Only two years later, after the end of the war, the next accident would take place as two trains collided at the above-ground Northwood station due to heavy fog on December 31. One of the train drivers hadn't seen the danger signal due to the fog, and the resulting crash resulted in three deaths. The next year, a train driver suffered a heart attack and hit the buffers after the train's dead man's handle failed to activate, but no one save the driver died. And while this couldn't have been helped, a driver error in 1953 resulted in twelve deaths after a signal failed and one train collided into the rear of another on the Central Line near Stratford. As the 1950s came to a close, fires started by electrical short circuits in trains on the Central Line caused the death of one person in 1958 and no fatalities in a similar fire in 1960.

Terrorism began to rear its ugly head again in the 1970s, with two bombs found in 1973 planted by the IRA that fortunately didn't explode. 1975, however, saw a bomb detonated outside of Green Park station that killed one and injured thirty. The year also proved deadly for another reason, as the Moorgate Tube Crash saw a southbound Northern City Line train fail to stop and crash into its end wall. Forty-three people died in the crash, the largest number of peacetime Tube fatalities, and no reason why the driver failed to stop was ever uncovered. The legacy of Moorgate was to introduce the "Moorgate protection," a system that automatically stops a train from moving too fast.

A number of IRA bombings and crashes continued into the 1980s, but by far, the worst disasters to occur during this decade were caused by fires in the Tube stations. On November 23, 1984, Oxford Circus station reported a fire that had begun in a materials store at the south end of the northbound Victoria Line platform where construction was being done to modernize the station. The station was evacuated, and while no one was killed, fourteen were taken to the hospital after suffering smoke inhalation. Believing that smoking materials getting into the store was responsible for the fire, a smoking ban took effect from that point forward. However, this was unable to stop another fire on November 18, 1987, at King's Cross station when a passenger dropped a lit match into the escalators. The escalators still had wooden parts; they caught fire and resulted in the deaths of thirty-one people and much stricter enforcement of the smoking ban.

As the 1990s dawned, the IRA renewed its attacks on the Underground from 1991 to 1993 with no reported injuries. However, with the Good Friday agreement in 1998, no further acts of violence from the IRA occurred. Several derailments were reported from 1999 to 2004, but safety measures enacted in previous years prevented any serious injuries. The London Underground's next travesty would befall it on July 7, 2005, when a series of coordinated terrorist attacks struck commuters during the morning rush hour. The country's first Islamic terrorist attack since the 1988 bombing of Pan Am Flight 103, at least three bombs were set off on trains and one on a double-decker bus that resulted in fifty-two deaths (not counting the bombers themselves). More attacks were attempted on July 21 but resulted in no casualties.

After this, there are fortunately few other incidents to report. The Mile End derailment in 2007 only resulted in minor injuries, and the terrorist attack on September 15, 2017, at Parsons Green station produced no fatalities. One can hope that as time goes on, safety and security will continue to improve and ensure that no other loss of life occurs on London's largest transport service.

WATFORD JUNCTION
WATFORD (HIGH STREET)
BUSHEY AND OXHEY
CARPENDERS PARK
HATCH END FOR PINNER
HEADSTONE LANE
HARROW & WEALDSTONE
KENTON
STANMORE
CANONS PARK
KINGSBURY
PRESTON ROAD
NEASDEN
DOLLIS HILL
NORTH WEMBLEY
WEMBLEY PARK
WEMBLEY FOR SUDBURY
STONEBRIDGE PARK
HARLESDEN
WILLESDEN JUNCTION
KENSAL GREEN
QUEENS PARK
KILBURN PARK
MAIDA VALE
WARWICK AVENUE
WILLESDEN GREEN
KILBURN & BRONDESBURY
WEST HAMPSTEAD
FINCHLEY ROAD
SWISS COTTAGE
MARLBORO ROAD
ST. JOHNS WOOD
EDGWARE
BURNT OAK (WATLING)
COLINDALE
HENDON CENTRAL
BRENT
GOLDERS GREEN
HAMPSTEAD
BELSIZE PARK
CHALK FARM
HIGHGATE
TUFNELL PARK
KENTISH TOWN
CAMDEN TOWN
MORNINGTON CRESCENT
EUSTON
HOLLOWAY ROAD
CALEDONIAN ROAD
LATIMER ROAD
WESTBOURNE PARK
ROYAL OAK
MARYLEBONE
LADBROKE GROVE
BISHOPS ROAD
EDGWARE ROAD
BAKER STREET
GREAT PORTLAND ST.
EUSTON SQUARE
EAST ACTON
BAYSWATER
PADDINGTON
PRAED STREET
REGENTS PARK
WARREN STREET
RUSSELL SQUARE
WOOD LANE
GOODGE STREET
UXBRIDGE ROAD
NOTTING HILL GATE
LANCASTER GATE
BOND STREET
HOLBORN
HOLLAND PARK
QUEENS ROAD
MARBLE ARCH
OXFORD CIRCUS
TOTTENHAM COURT ROAD
BRITISH MUSEUM
COVENT GARDEN
PICCADILLY
DOVER STREET
LEICESTER SQUARE
ADDISON ROAD
HIGH STREET KENSINGTON
HYDE PARK CORNER
STRAND
TEMPLE
KNIGHTSBRIDGE
BROMPTON ROAD
TRAFALGAR SQUARE
CHARING CROSS
HAMMERSMITH
BARONS COURT
EARLS COURT
GLOUCESTER ROAD
WESTMINSTER
VICTORIA
WEST KENSINGTON
SOUTH KENSINGTON
SLOANE SQUARE
ST. JAMES PARK
WEST BROMPTON
WALHAM GREEN
PARSONS GREEN
PUTNEY BRIDGE
EAST PUTNEY
SOUTHFIELDS
WIMBLEDON PARK
WIMBLEDON
CLAPHAM SOUTH
BALHAM
TOOTING BROADWAY
COLLIERS WOOD
SOUTH WIMBLEDON (MERTON)
MORDEN

A HISTORY OF HARRY BECK'S ICONIC TUBE MAP

London's history is filled with historical figures who were just doing a job or once had an idea that turned into something bigger than they ever intended. Henry C Beck was a simple draftsman who thought the London Underground's Tube map was too complicated and could be easier to understand if it looked more like an electrical diagram. This led to a global standard that most transport networks now follow. Despite this, there was a fight to get credit for his creation from London Transport.

The London Underground railway system, always referred to as "The Tube," was the world's first such system and began with the opening in 1863 of the Metropolitan Line. The train was pulled through the tunnels by a steam engine fueled with coal, and the carriages were lit by gas lights. The system was intended for transporting workers, and indeed, with all the smoke and ash filling the tunnels and the stations, few other people were willing to use the early trains. Nonetheless, other lines soon followed, with the District and the Circle Lines by 1884. These early lines were shallow, vented by shafts in the walls extending to the surface, which can still be seen at Baker Street station, and extended up to 50 miles out into the countryside, where much of the working-class lived.

Fully underground lines with electric trains began in 1890 with the City and South London Line, and by the early 20th century, an extensive network of different companies, linked by marketing agreements, ran the system. During WWI, and again in WWII, the stations were used as underground shelters against bombing raids. After WWI, with government funding and support, the system was further expanded, and in 1933 all the underground trains and the above-ground bus and tram services were merged into the London Passenger Transport Board (LPTB). Following the election of the Labour government after WWII on a platform of nationalization of industry, the LPTB was nationalized.

In the early days of the system, each separate company printed a map of its own line showing the various stations. But in 1908, under the early marketing agreements that were made, a joint map was published, and at the same time the 'UNDERGROUND' term was promoted and displayed prominently across the top of the early maps. These first maps were geographically accurate, showing streets and other features. As a result, showing enough detail for the central area meant leaving outlying sections of the lines of the map completely. Leslie MacDonald Gill was a cartographer and graphic designer, connected through his brother to the Arts and Crafts Movement. In 1913, he produced a map of the system in a humorous style, called the Wunderground Map, which hung in all the stations. His style of combining accuracy with cartoon-style illustrations is still seen today on many maps.

THE TUBE MAP IN THE 1920'S

Max, as he was known, abandoned geographic accuracy for clarity and entertainment, but simultaneously much more sparse maps, showing just the stations on a straight line, were being produced and displayed in stations and on platforms. These were drawn by George Dow, employed by the London and North Eastern Railway and a railway historian in his own right.

Around 1930, an engineering draftsman at the London Underground Signals Office, called Henry Charles Beck, or more often simply 'Harry,' sat down in his spare time and devised a linear plan of the whole system, showing the interrelationships, but not the actual positions, of the underground stations and lines. His direct inspiration was the electrical circuit diagrams he was working on, which simply showed connections, without any scale. Many people also believe he was influenced by Max's linear diagrams of the individual lines and Gill's introduction of graphics.

HARRY BECK

Believing that he was correct in thinking that people only wanted to know where the stations were, and where to change lines, Beck approached Frank Pick, an executive at London Underground, who was the person who commissioned Max Gill's Wunderground map. Pick, and others were skeptical, but Beck persisted, and a trial printing of 500 maps appeared at a few stations in 1932. This was also to become the last year that the previous geographic maps, at this period being designed by F. H. Stingemore, were to appear. Beck had done all his work in his own time and was paid 15 guineas for the artwork of the pamphlet and poster forms of his design. A guinea was a sum equivalent to one pound plus one shilling (one-20th of a pound), and Beck's 15guineas would be worth between one and five thousand pounds today, depending on the conversion system used. There is some dispute as to whether, in fact, any payment was made at all.

Beck's new map proved an instant hit with the commuting public and 700,000 copies were printed and distributed throughout the system in 1933. That first printing was gone within a month, and much larger reprints quickly followed. For some time, Beck was employed on a freelance basis to update and amend the map, but in 1960 London Transport used an employee, Harold Hutchinson, to add the new Victoria Line to the map and began making other changes without consulting Beck. His name as the designer was removed from the bottom of the map. Five years of legal struggle followed as Beck tried to get control of the map back, but when his wife's mental health began to suffer Beck withdrew from the battle, defeated.

Beck had left London Underground in 1947 and eked out a living as a freelance designer and teacher until his death in 1974. He continued to make changes to his original design and submit them to London Transport, only to have them rejected. He continued to privately make modifications and sketches for the rest of his life.

Following the split with Beck, a new designer, Paul Garbutt, was employed to update the map. He is responsible for the familiar 'flask' shape of the Central Line. Garbutt had actually produced his first version privately and presented it to London Underground, as he found the Hutchinson map so bad. Beck was much more sympathetic to Garbutt's design. It was Garbutt who carried the map into its modern version, working on it for 20 years. Later maps added features such as the surface rail and light-rail systems of the city, and in 2002 when a fare system using zones was introduced, these were added to the map too.

THE TUBE MAP TODAY

In 1997, Beck's reputation was rehabilitated, and his name now appears again on all Underground maps, as the original conceiver of the map. His map has been voted second-favorite British design, after Concorde. The style of design has been copied by railway and underground systems worldwide. The irony is that the modern Tube Map (pictured left) has now become confusing again with the addition of the new London Overground and other new lines.

SITES TO VISIT AND FURTHER RESEARCH

- Beck's work on this and other maps can be seen in the Beck Gallery at the London Transport Museum, in the Covent Garden Piazza, WC2E. The Museum is open until 6 p.m. every day and is well worth a visit for anyone interested in London's fascinating transport history.

- There is a blue plaque on the house where Beck was born, 14 Wesley Road, Leyton, E10. The nearest Tube stop is Leyton Station, on the Central Line.
- There is a commemorative plaque to Beck, and an early design by him, at Finchley Central Tube station.

THE TEN BUSIEST TUBE STATIONS AND THEIR HISTORIES

Transport for London estimates that 1.37 billion people ride the Tube every year, moving through the network's 249 miles of track and 270 stations. And while thousands of people pass through every day going to work, home, out, or just sightseeing, they don't often reflect on the history of the stations. If you stop for a moment, we think you'll find that London's ten busiest Underground stations are some of the most fascinating. Numbers are based on data collected from 2016 by Transport for London.

PADDINGTON – 49.48 MILLION

Paddington was built as the London Terminus for the Great Western Railway, and the Great Western Hotel (now Hilton London Paddington) was constructed along with it. The Underground lines were added in 1863. Perhaps the most famous aspect of the station comes not from its trains but the Paddington Bear children's books created by Michael Bond. Today, a statue of Paddington Bear on Platform 1.

CANARY WHARF – 54.79 MILLION

One of the newest stations on this list, Canary Wharf was a business district that was constructed to revitalize the London Docklands in the 1980s. However, the area was pretty poorly served by public transport, and the Jubilee Line Extension was constructed in the 1990s to accommodate the commuters. The station opened officially in 1999, and the area's success is the reason why it is such a busy Tube station. Canary Wharf is also home to the longest escalator in the Underground and has appeared in notable films such as 28 Days Later and Star Wars: Rogue One.

BANK & MONUMENT – 64.26 MILLION

Bank & Monument actually refer to two interlinked stations named for the Bank of England and the Monument to the Great Fire of London, respectively. They were constructed as part of the Metropolitan Railway and District Railway in 1884 and eventually became the Circle Line in 1949. One of the more tragic events in the stations' history was during the London Blitz when a German bomb hit the booking hall, and the explosion traveled downwards to the platforms.

STRATFORD – 67.05 MILLION

Stratford was constructed in 1839 as part of the Eastern Counties Railways and today is a multi-level interchange for the Underground, Crossrail, the Overground, and National Rail. The station has no connection to Stratford-upon-Avon, and to distinguish it, it is sometimes referred to as Stratford (London). Stratford is preparing for the future when full Crossrail service replaces TfL Rail in 2019, making the station part of the most advanced rail network in the UK. Stratford also has the shortest escalator at 4.1 meters.

LONDON BRIDGE – 70.74 MILLION

Named for the nearby London Bridge, the station was built in 1836 as part of the London & Croydon Railway. While the London & Greenwich Railways opened stations before L&C opened London Bridge, those stations' closings make London Bridge the oldest active Underground station in the network. Both London Bridge station entrances were damaged during the Blitz. With the more recent construction of the Shard, London Bridge Station got an overhaul with a new entrance and roof on the terminal level.

LIVERPOOL STREET – 71.61 MILLION

Liverpool Street was constructed to be a new terminus in the city, one for the Great Eastern Railway. As with Paddington, a hotel was constructed as part of the terminus known as the Great Eastern Hotel (now known as the Andaz London Liverpool Street). At first, it was thought that the station was a waste of money, but it wasn't ten years before the station was at capacity and needed expansion. The station has a couple of monuments to World War I and World War II and was one of the stations attacked on 7 July 2005.

OXFORD CIRCUS – 83.26 MILLION

Found at the junction of Regent Street and Oxford Street, the Oxford Circus Station was opened as part of the Central Line in 1900. The Bakerloo Line station opened six years later, and both of them are Grade II listed buildings. Ten years ago, Oxford Circus went through a major renovation that removed the 1980s murals and replaced them with white tile similar to what the station had when it opened. One attraction that garners much attention, as well as a lot of Tube travelers who work there, is BBC Broadcasting House.

VICTORIA – 83.5 MILLION

London Victoria Station was constructed in 1860 and was meant to serve the Chatham and Brighton Lines. The two parts of the station were built two years apart, and as such, have always felt like two stations rather than one. Victoria was one of the last stations to see steam trains, which were eventually phased out in the 1960s. One of the most innovative aspects of the station was its Gatwick Express train, which included check-in desks for the airlines at the platform. With over 80 million people using the station each year, Victoria has been scheduled for upgrades to its service.

KINGS CROSS ST. PANCRAS – 95.03 MILLION

King's Cross St. Pancras is one of the oldest in the Underground, opening in 1863 as part of the Metropolitan Railway. Its location and connection to the King's Cross Railway Station make it the second-busiest Underground station in London. In possibly the worst tragedy in the Tube's history, the wooden parts of the station's escalators caught fire and resulted in the deaths of thirty-one people. The fire resulted in a major renovation of the station in the 1980s. The above rail station is most associated with the Harry Potter series as the gateway to the Hogwarts Express.

WATERLOO – 100.36 MILLION

Seeing 100.36 million users in 2016, Waterloo Station easily takes the cake for the busiest in the whole Underground. It was constructed in 1898 as part of the Waterloo & City Railway, now known as the Waterloo & City Line. Part of the reason for its use is that it connects four different lines, which besides Waterloo & City Line, includes the Jubilee, Northern, and Bakerloo lines. The area around the station is also home to several major landmarks, including the London Eye, the Imperial War Museum, and Southbank Centre, amongst others.

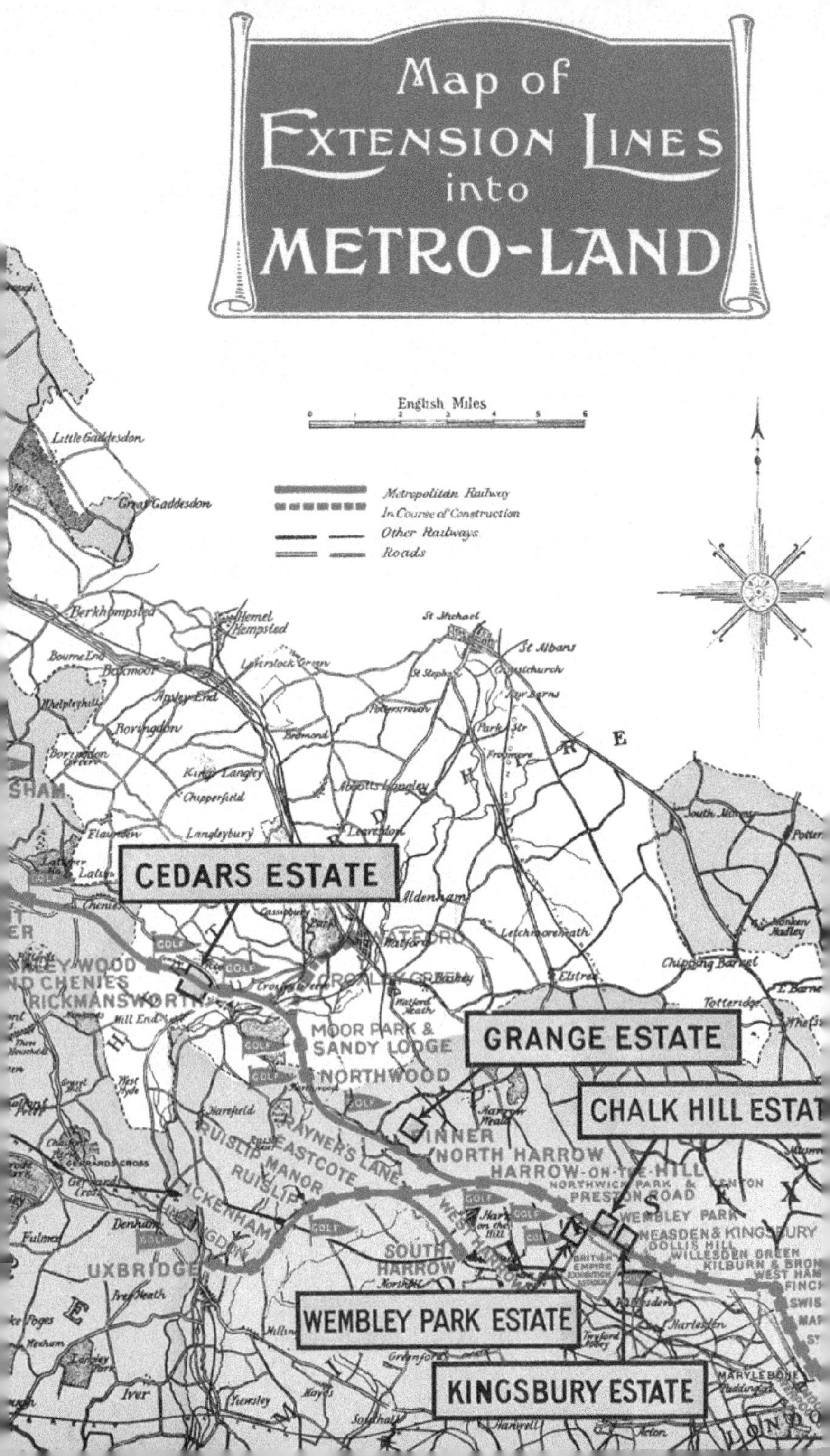
Map of
EXTENSION LINES
into
METRO-LAND
English Miles
Metropolitan Railway
In Course of Construction
Other Railways
Roads
CEDARS ESTATE
GRANGE ESTATE
CHALK HILL ESTAT
WEMBLEY PARK ESTATE
KINGSBURY ESTATE
Little Gaddesdon
Great Gaddesdon
Berkhampsted
Hemel Hempsted
St Michael
St Albans
Boxmoor
Kings Langley
Chipperfield
Langleybury
Abbotts Langley
Aldenham
Watford
Leverstock Green
Bedmond
Letchmoreheath
Elstree
Chipping Barnet
Totteridge
South Mimms
CHORLEY WOOD
AND CHENIES
RICKMANSWORTH
MOOR PARK &
SANDY LODGE
NORTHWOOD
PINNER
NORTH HARROW
HARROW-ON-THE-HILL
NORTHWICK PARK & KENTON
PRESTON ROAD
WEMBLEY PARK
NEASDEN & KINGSBURY
DOLLIS HILL
WILLESDEN GREEN
RAYNER'S LANE
EASTCOTE
RUISLIP MANOR
RUISLIP
ICKENHAM
HILLINGDON
UXBRIDGE
SOUTH HARROW
WEST HARROW
Harefield
Denham
Gerrards Cross
Iver
Yiewsley
Southall
Hanwell
Acton
Harlesden
Greenford
MARYLEBONE
Paddington

A GUIDE TO METROLAND – THE SUBURBAN EXPANSION OF LONDON BROUGHT ON BY THE TUBE

Also known as Metro-land, this suburban area northwest of London was a major project by the railway to transform unused land into a series of residential communities. Metroland wasn't the first time a rail company was instrumental in growing London. In truth, the continued influx of people from the countryside to London in the 19th Century had caused the city's metropolitan area to expand exponentially. However, this growth was more haphazard and unplanned, sprawling up around the railways that were able to carry people from Greater London into the heart of the City.

With Metroland, it was different. Utilizing extra land granted to the Metropolitan Railway, the railway developed its own planning commission and promoted new homes that would make it easy for families to live in the country and work in the city. Unfortunately, the grand scheme was not to last as the Metropolitan Railways was eventually absorbed into the London Passenger Transport Board, the predecessor of the modern Transport for London. In this article, we'll look at the beginnings of Metroland, what made up the villages, how the areas around them grew with London, its advertisements and appearances in media, and how Metroland is today.

THE BUILDING OF METRO-LAND

The Metropolitan Railway had been around since 1863, when its first trains were pulled by steam-driven locomotives, and its passenger cars were still lit by gas lamps. It ran from the heart of the City of London at Farringdon Station, through Middlesex, and eventually reached all the way out to Buckinghamshire. The Met, as it was known, as created by a series of acts in 1854, 1855, 1856, and 1860. This conglomeration of laws had in its clauses the ability for the railway to keep the surplus land it didn't use instead of being forced to sell it.

At the turn of the century, the Met needed to find new ways to raise revenue. Rather than dispose of the surplus land for profit, it seized upon the idea to create a customer base by building villages on that land. Robert Selbie, the General Manager, came up with the idea in 1912 to form a company that would decide how best to develop the properties instead of the railway's Surplus Lands Committee, but his plans were put on hold when World War I began in 1914.

After the war was over, the Met sought a legal opinion on what it could do with the land only to be told that it had the legal ability to hold the land, but not develop it. In response to this opinion, the Met formed Metropolitan Railway Country Estates Ltd. (MCRE) in 1919. Using this company, it took the lands that it owned and crafted several estates and villages including Kingsby Garden Village, Harrow Garden Village, and the Cecil Park, Grange, and Wembley Park Estates in the Town of Pinner.

In the post-war housing boom, the states proved quite a success both in terms of successfully housing new residents as well as increasing the Met's ticket sales. Between 1921 and 1924, the Met's ticket sales rose 700% as residents of these new estates journeyed from Greater London into the city. Each area where MRCE built estates resulted in a population boom for surrounding communities. Harrow Weald's population went from 5,000 to 11,000 while Pinner went from 3,000 to 23,000 overtime. By the time the Metropolitan Railway became part of the London Passenger Transport Board in 1933, it had left a major impact on Northwest London. LPTB had little interest in continuing the scheme, and future development was left up to other private firms and local councils.

THE VILLAGES AND ESTATES

Harrow Garden Village

Harrow Garden Village has unofficially been referred to as the "Capital of Metro-land." Established in 1925 and built around the Rayners Lane Underground Station in the Borough of Harrow, the village was the MCRE's flagship development. The majority of the development was represented by the semi-detached Tudor-style homes that would be the face of Metro-land with sixteen different styles of homes all designed by builder E.S. Reid. The development even included Longfield School, and Rayners Lane Baptist Church were also part of Harrow Garden Village from the beginning. Station Parade, a shopping center, soon followed along with residents that boosted the borough's population up to 11,000. The area around Harrow Garden Village continued to develop in subsequent years, transforming Harrow from a country borough into a true suburb.

Wembley – Chalkhill and Wembley Park Estates

Wembley Park in the Borough of Brent was once part of a large landscaped estate in the 18th Century. In 1880, the Metropolitan Railways expanded out into Middlesex and cut through the former estate, buying up forty-seven acres and later the estate itself. While the Met would sit on the unused land for years, by 1915, it would become part of the MCRE's proposed Metro-land developments. The pre-existing pleasure gardens and nearby golf courses made a large part of the advertising for the Wembley Park development in 1924. Chalkhill was one of the first estates MCRE built in Wembley Park. TV studios, a cinema, and a pool soon followed. The area was actually quite prosperous until the 1960s and 1970s when new Council Estates ended up becoming havens for crime. The decline continued until Chalkhill was redeveloped in the 1990s, and the rest of Wembley Park followed in the early 21st Century.

Pinner – Cecil Park and Grange Estates

Also part of the Borough of Harrow, the Town of Pinner began as a hamlet that was in existence no later than 900 AD, with the first recorded mention in 1291. The town's name comes from the River Pinner that runs right through its center. The oldest part of Pinner was centered around St. John the Baptist Parrish Church, which dates back to the 14th Century, and there were a few homes in the area before the Metropolitan Railway came to the town. Beginning in 1923, it developed the Cecil Park and Grange Lane estates while encouraging several others such as Pinnerwood and Elm Park Court, amongst others. These developments helped Pinner grow by roughly 20,000 people over a few decades. Today, Pinner is considered a wealthy part of Harrow and has held the city's longest annual street fair since 1336.

Rickmansworth – Cedars Estate

Rickmansworth was founded along with five other manors as part of the Abbey of St. Albans in 793 AD. After the Dissolution of the Monasteries, not much of note occurred in Ricksmanworth until the Metropolitan Railway came through the area in the 19th Century. By the 1920s, Ricksmanworth (or "Ricky" as the locals call it) was quickly becoming a suburban commuter town thanks to Metro-land. While many other Metroland developments were almost exclusively Tudor-style homes, Ricksmanworth's prior history and development during the Victorian period means there's a greater diversity of the homes in this community. Other than that, there isn't much to report on Rickmansworth although it was one of the communities featured in Sir John Betjeman's 1973 documentary

Metro-land on the MCRE's housing estates.

Neasden – Kingsbury Garden Village

Falling so close to Wembley, Neasden was a simple countryside hamlet for centuries, only having a number of small cottages, farms, a pub, a smitty, and other simple signs of civilization. Even by the early Victorian period, a little over one-hundred people lived in Neasden, though that certainly changed when the Metropolitan Railway opened its Dudding Hill Station in 1875. By 1891, the population was in the 500s but would begin to grow even more when MCRE started laying out the streets for Kingsbury Garden Village, one of its first developments that would be part of Metroland. Unfortunately, the prosperity that Metroland brought to Neasden was not to last, and the area declined after World War II. However, it has survived and maintained a diverse culture that includes the Neasden Temple, the largest Hindu Temple outside of India. As Neasden continues into the future, its history as one of the earliest parts of Metroland is almost as forgotten as the village itself, though its reawakening is always on the horizon.

METROLAND IN MEDIA

Some of the earliest media associated with Metro-land were the adverts used to convince Londoners to move to the developments. Like cheery propaganda posters, they displaced lovely Tudor homes, landmarks such as the British Exhibition Centre, and idyllic suburban life. The image of a young woman picking flowers surrounded by greenery certainly would have appealed to Londoners as a contrast to the drab gray of the city. Other posters focused on the local train stations that could easily take them from their country homes to work and back. The Metropolitan Railway even advertised its terminus at Baker Street as "The Gateway to Metro-land".

As Metroland began to take root in the public consciousness, the developments worked their way into media as early as the end of World War I. It was about that time that George Sims penned the line "I know a land where the wildflowers grow/ Near, near at hand if by train you go,/Metroland, Metroland!" into one of his songs. By the 1930s, Evelyn Waugh was using the term in his novels Decline and Fall, Vile Bodies, and A Handful of Dust. More songs soon followed such as "My Little Metro-land Home" all the way up to "Queensbury Station" by The Magoo Brothers in 1988, which makes many references to the area.

Metroland has had its share of appearances across film and television as well. During the 1960s, the popular sci-fi spy series The Avengers often had its stories taking place in Metro-land communities. Such was the number of episodes that took place here that, during the show's run, Metroland was nicknamed Avengerland. In 1973, Poet Laureate John Betjeman made his famous documentary Metro-Land, taking a tour of the various developments and communities that sprang up along the Metropolitan Railway. The documentary was critically very successful, and to this day, any attempts at revitalization often invoke Metro-Land as a means to conjure up images of the region's heyday.

Shortly afterward, another television series, The Good Life, aired in the UK that took place in a Metro-land community and focused on a couple who decided to "go back to nature" in their own modern neighborhood. 1997 saw Metroland immortalized on screen in a film of the same name. Starring Christian Bale and Emily Watson, it was based on the 1980s novel by Julian Barnes. The pair play a husband and wife living in Metroland when the sudden reappearance of Bale's childhood friend causes him to remember his carefree past and question his life choices. Ultimately, Bale chooses his family and happiness in the British suburbs, perhaps reinforcing the ideal of suburban contentment that Metroland evoked.

In each representation, from the original ads to more modern film, Metroland continued to be portrayed as the perfect suburban life. Work in the city, home in the country, and everything that most Londoners in the 20th Century could have wanted. Even while communities faced development problems, economic decline, and even crime, the image crafted by the media for Metroland remained upbeat and pastoral.

AFTER METROLAND

Even though Metro-land as a marketing gimmick went away with the Metropolitan Railway's absorption into the London Passenger Transport Board, the effects of the Met's development remained. The Metropolitan became yet another of the Underground's many lines. LPTB stopped running cargo freight up the Metropolitan all freight was transferred to the London and North Eastern Railway. The Board also closed lines that split off and ran to Brill and Verney Junction, effectively ending the Met at Amersham and Chesham and the rest of the line being run by steam locomotives. Despite this, the Underground stations along with the estates actually saw enhancements including new trains and an expansion of the lines at Harrow, making for an even better commute for Metro-land residents.

The change in the use of the railways wasn't the only thing that was different after the Board took over, abandoning the estates and any new residential development plans were scrapped. Architects and developers started to frown on suburbia following World War II. The concept had become dated and uniform. No one was interested in mock-Tudor style or homes that all looked the same. Yet suburbia still held a draw to the English heart, as noted by J.M. Richards in his book The Castles on the Ground when he said "for all the alleged deficiencies of suburban taste…it holds for ninety out of a hundred Englishman an appeal which cannot be explained away as some strange instance of mass aberration." Even as the word "suburbia" fell into disfavor, "Metroland" continued to be used as a way to describe these outlying communities.

Over time, though, the idyllic countryside that the Met had promised began to fall by the wayside as London's urbanity spread further into the surrounding counties. Where Harrow had once been regarded as the capital of Metro-land, a pastoral idea of suburban life, it found itself surrounded by greater London. Wembley Park, meanwhile, ceased to be identifiable from the rest of the city. This was no more evident than when the Olympics and later the World Cup came to Wembley, signifying that this area was no mere development anymore. Wembley became a major center of London events as Wembley Stadium also played host to a papal visit, Live Aid, the Euro Cup, and more.

As mentioned before, some of the estates and their villages didn't fair as well. Neasden, in particular, experienced a steady decline, especially as city traffic grew with the populace. Congestion got so bad that the North Circular Road was constructed, and after the war, continued to grow such that an underpass was built which had the effect of bisecting Neasden and cutting off pedestrian access to one of its largest shopping centers. Chalkhill had new estate housing built that was designed with many skyways that connected the buildings and was initially praised for its innovation. However, the housing utopia slipped into dystopia as those same walkways in the Chalkhill Estate became convenient escape routes for criminals, aiding in the area's urban decay. The continued deterioration of the estate conditions ultimately led to its demolition and redevelopment. In fact, redevelopment was a scheme in store for most of the Metroland estates as the 21st Century dawned. While wealthier areas continued to flourish, gentrification would soon ensure that the other Met communities would soon join their success.

METROLAND TODAY

In the present, the dream of Metroland has long since faded. Few, if any, are around who remember life before London's underground railways came under government control and fewer who knew the opening of Metroland's estates. Forty-five years have passed since Betjeman made his classic documentary and areas like Neasden, Harrow, and Wembley have continued to change in his absence. In the decades since some of Metroland's communities have since been swallowed up by an ever-expanding London. Others that fell onto hard times have since seen revitalization thanks to redevelopment. Yes, gentrification has come to Metroland, and the suburbia will never be the same—again.

Harrow and Wembley have always been more on the affluent side, even going as far back as the start of Metroland. Harrow School is one of Britain's boarding schools that exemplifies wealth and privilege ever since it was founded under a Royal Charter from Queen Elizabeth I in 1572. Homes not built as part of suburban Metroland can go in the millions of pounds. However, this is mostly confined to the northern part of the borough, and southern Harrow has more working-class people. In fact, many communities in the area have problems with overcrowding and "beds in sheds" or outbuildings hastily built to house lower-income persons. The borough today is also a very diverse one, with approximately 64% of residents belonging to Black or Minority Ethnic communities. This was no better represented than in the council's annual festival, Under One Sky, which started in 2005 as a means of celebrating this diversity, but was canceled beginning in 2014 due to funding concerns.

Nearby Neasden is one of the prime examples of the gentrification that's taken over parts of Metroland. The 1990s saw both the demolition of the historic Grange Tavern for new flats as well as the construction of the Neasden Temple. The shopping center that was harmed by the expansion of the North Circular Road was redeveloped in 2004. In both Harrow and Neasden, newer, blocky apartment buildings have been going up to accommodate those persons who can no longer afford to live close to Central London, while those in the more affluent neighborhoods have moved into the expensive condos being built closer to the business and financial districts of London. Chalkhill still has its issues, especially with drugs and gangs, but since the 1990s, the estate has been redeveloped to alleviate the worst of the community's crime problems, and just outside the estate are single-family homes and duplexes alongside newer apartment buildings—all within view of the rebuilt Wembley Stadium.

This is the new Metroland, one that is a mixture of cultures, incomes, and age groups. These renovated homes and new apartments are providing homes to immigrant communities seeking a better life, young professionals who can no longer afford the city, and new families who want the homes and yards to grow. While a lot of developers are more interested in tearing down and building something new, plenty of Londoners are looking at something old and making it new again. As much as new apartments might appeal to younger generations, cramped lofts with high rents are what everyone is looking for in life. For the rest of us, the semis of Metroland offer an appeal that escapes modern development firms. These homes offer space to unfurl your wings and live in a community rather than a mixed-use maze, to be closer to schools than to clubs.

And thus, Metroland has come full circle. The homes that once called to new families and working people are doing so again. Neasden, Wembley Park, Chalkhill, Rickmansworth, and more are bridging the gap between urbanized London and suburban Greater London. As northwest London continues its march towards redevelopment, there is still a place for the homes that the Metropolitan Railway constructed. Today, as when they were new, these houses serve the purpose for which they were intended—providing homes and communities to all manner of Londoners.

DWYCH

THE TUBE DURING WORLD WAR II

Millions of people travel on the London Underground every day, but few of them have ever taken shelter there or know fully how their everyday commute played such a large role in World War II. Of course, most people know about Londoners taking shelter in the stations during the London Blitz or secret bunkers are hidden away from the danger of bombs, but there's even more than that. As it turns out, the Underground played a vital part in Britain's war effort in many areas: sheltering the people, providing leaders with a base of operations, and even producing the weapons that the nation used to defend itself.

To start off, the idea of the London Underground as a bomb shelter wasn't a new one by 1940. During World War I, German zeppelins and Gotha airplanes had bombed the city and forced people to take shelter in the tunnels. At this time, the Underground lines were mostly owned and run by separate companies, all of which were merged together with the bus system in 1933 to create London Transport. Additionally, the government had taken the position between the wars that the use of the stations as air raid shelters should be actively discouraged.

To that extent, when the bombing started, the Ministry of Home Security sought to build about ten air raid shelters throughout the city with the facilities and bunks to house thousands of people. However, while ten were planned, only eight were actually constructed, and what's more, while they were adjacent to the Tube stations, most of them were used by the government until five were opened to the public in 1944.

As a result, a majority of Londoners seeking shelter continued to use the Underground. Meanwhile, a test of the air raid siren and anti-aircraft missiles on 3 March 1943 led to a panicked rush on the Bethnal Green Station for shelter, which ultimately resulted in the deaths of 173 people. It easily became the highest civilian loss of life during the war (as well as being arguably the single worst disaster in the Underground's history). While the government at first attempted to prevent the use of the stations and tunnels as shelters, it eventually relented as thousands continued to use them anyway, and some people would even squat in the tunnels to sell prime spots to the highest bidders. The government then started regulating and policing the stations as well as handing out tickets to prevent overcrowding.

The government also made use of certain tube stations for its administrative offices and for the military during World War II. Most notably, the Brompton Road Tube Station, which had permanently shut in 1934, was reopened during the war as a station for the 1st Anti-Aircraft Division to defend the city. The front of the station was bricked up and turned into offices, while the tunnels became the division's operations center. It was subsequently given to the Territorial Army after the war, and the main building was demolished in 1972. When Blue Peter paid the remaining parts of the station a visit in 2000, they still found maps and other war memorabilia in place. What's more, even the Americans were able to use some portions of the Tube as a base, including the Goodge Street Station, which served as a base for General Eisenhower.

South Kensington was also used by the government for various purposes, from a signaling school to storing equipment used to study time-delay bombs.

As the Blitz had done significant damage to factories and other key pieces of British infrastructure, some of it was relocated to the Underground to protect from further attacks. Several stations were converted to manufacturing of aircraft components and other necessary items for the war effort, such as Earl's Court and Gants Hill. The latter of the two had an entire section of the Underground converted to its use between that station and the Leytonstone station, even utilizing the tracks to move people and components from one end of the factory to the other. In yet another use, the long-disused Aldwych station, which is often now used for filming scenes in need of an older station, housed plenty of great British treasures. The British Museum housed a number of exhibits and works of art there, including the Elgin Marbles, in order to protect these national treasures from the Nazi war machine.

Thus, beyond the uses that many people know about, the Underground served Britain during World War II in a variety of roles. It not only sheltered London's citizens, but also Britain's great works. It aided the war by providing the British military and its allies with a place to operate as well as giving its factories work space to continue making vital components to fighting the war.

A BRIEF HISTORY OF THE LONDON OVERGROUND

A very recent addition to Transport for London, the London Overground isn't a Bizarro-mirror-universe copy of the London Underground. However, it is very much what it says on the tin and where the Underground is a below-ground rail system, the Overground is more of a metropolitan train service. The Overground is what is known as a suburban rail network that carries residents of London's suburbs into the city center. Also, unlike the London Underground, the Overground essentially goes straight into the city and back and did not move around much within the city limits in its earlier years, meaning riders needed to use other public transport to get to their final destinations.

The idea for the Overground originated in the 1970s with a concept called Ringrail. The original proposal called for a rail network that closely followed the old North London Line with stations at twenty-minute intervals. However, there wasn't much interest from Prime Minister Harold Wilson's government nor from National Rail, the latter of which had little interest in running railways that only served small local networks. Fortunately for North Londoners, the Greater London Council felt differently and sponsored two lines in 1979 and 1984.

These lines eventually gave way to the Silverlink in 1997, a metro railway service owned by National Express. Unfortunately, Silverlink did not do a great job managing the railway, and the line suffered from neglect over the ten-year period of the franchise. Commuters often complained of unkempt stations, overcrowded trains, and unreliable service, with trains often canceled before they were due to arrive. A London Assembly report actually called the Starlink service "shabby, unreliable, unsafe, and overcrowded." Perhaps unsurprisingly, the Department for Transport announced in 2004 a review of the rail industry in the United Kingdom, and Transport for London proposed taking control of all rail services operating in and around London.

The Department for Transport took the proposal to heart. In 2006, the Department for Transport transferred management of metro rail services to Transport for London. Shortly afterward on September 5, TfL announced the rebranding of Silverlink as the London Overground. In 2007, TfL did not renew National Express's franchise and instead awarded the franchise to a joint venture of Lainig Rail and MTR. TfL also broke up the previous North London Railway network and reintegrated it into the existing metro network, as well as updating the rolling stock trains. It also made sure to give the infrastructure a significant upgrade and refurbish the stations to improve the quality of the service. TfL also introduced Oyster to all 55 stations when the rebranded service launched.

In 2010, TfL gave the Overground its first major extension with the South London line. Transport for London moved the line over from the London Underground after the completion of Phase 1 of its extension, increasing the Overground's reach down to West Croydon from its Dalston station. In 2012, the Overground became an orbital network with the line extended from Surrey Quays to Clapham Junction, finally tying what was once a fractured rail network together to improve service for commuters. In 2015, Liverpool Street to Enfield Town, Chesnut (via Seven Sisters), Chingford, and the Romford to Upminster service transferred from the East Anglia rail service and became part of the Overground.

What started as a simple commuter rail operating in the north and west London has grown into a sprawling and unified network. Today the Overground has 112 stations over six routes, appearing on the TfL map as an octopus with tentacles stretching out to cover London's major suburbs. Over the course of one year, from 2016 to 2017, the Overground had 189 million passenger journeys, proving it's an incredibly important part of London's transportation infrastructure.

LONDON UNDER: THAMES TUNNELS AND THEIR AMAZING HISTORIES

With all the tunnels under the River Thames, it might seem strange to think that it was once a nearly impossible feat of engineering. By the beginning of the 19th Century, the need to move cargo was becoming more important for Britain's economy, and London's bridges were too cramped with carriage and pedestrian traffic to expect to move that cargo quickly. The solution was then to go under the river, but that presented brand-new problems for the engineers. In fact, the Thames Tunnel, the first successful one under the river, took eighteen years to complete. Today, there are many tunnels that run under the river serving many different functions, from moving people to moving waste.

TREVITHICK'S TUNNEL

Before the Brunel's succeeded in their tunnel, Richard Trevithick made the first attempt at carving a tunnel out under the River Thames in 1807. However, while one side of the river had a base of clay that was perfect for tunneling, the other side was a mix of sand, gravel, quicksand, peat, and more that gave the project fits. Just 140 feet from the north bank, they hit quicksand and water, causing the pilot tunnel to flood. By that point, the project had already cost too much to continue and was abandoned.

THAMES TUNNEL

Begun in 1825, the Thames Tunnel was the project of famed engineers Marc Isambard Brunel and his son, Isambard Kingdom Brunel. To succeed where Trevithick failed, Marc Brunel adapted his methods to the soft ground and developed a tunneling shield that supported the structure of the tunnel until workers were able to excavate and support the tunnel. Isambard Brunel completed the project that connected Rotherhithe and Wapping in 1845. At first, it was primarily a pedestrian tunnel until purchased by the East London Railway and turned into a rail tunnel but eventually closed as other Underground and Overground lines became more prominent, though it was periodically reopened and used over the years. Closed for good, the Brunel Museum now exists at the entrance at Rotherhithe.

GREENWICH FOOT TUNNEL

Coming at the tail end of the century, the Greenwich Foot Tunnel began in 1899 and finished in 1902. It was designed by Alexander Binnie and commissioned by the London County Council to replace a ferry that helped workers get from South London to the docks. Repaired and refitted several times during its history, it still sees use by bicyclists and pedestrians.

BLACKWALL TUNNEL

Linking Tower Hamlets and Greenwich, Blackwall Tunnel was

first constructed from 1892-1897, then a second tunnel was added from 1960-1967. At the time the first tunnel was constructed, there wasn't much a path for people in East London to get over the river except a long route west to London Bridge. This tunnel was also designed by Binnie and commissioned by the LCC. When vehicle traffic became too much for the original tunnel, the second one was built in the 1960s. The Southern Tunnel gateway house is now Grade II listed, and Transport for London is championing the proposed Silvertown Tunnel to relieve congestion in Blackwall Tunnel.

CROSSRAIL TUNNEL

Crossrail is an Underground tunnel designed to link London with Berkshire, Buckinghamshire, and Essex. Construction on the central tunnel began in 2009, and a section of the line from Liverpool Street to Shenfield opened in 2015, with the rest of Crossrail expected to open in 2019. The idea of linking some of the home counties with London by rail has been around since the late-1940s but didn't become a reality until it was approved by TFL in 2007. It's now open and known as the Elizabeth Line.

THE UNDERGROUND

Speaking of train lines, we'd be amiss not to at least briefly mention the London Underground. This series of underground rail tunnels were the first of their kind when it opened in 1863. Several different railways operated the various lines until they all merged as the Underground in the early 20th Century. The District, Victoria, Northern, Bakerloo, and East London lines all run under the Thames, and the Underground sees approximately 4.8 million passenger journeys a day.

LEE TUNNEL

Not a normal tunnel and certainly not meant to move people, Lee Tunnel is actually the largest and deepest sewer in London. The tunnel was constructed as part of the London Tidewater Project and is designed to help make the river cleaner by 2020. At its deepest, it runs 260 feet deep, which is even deeper than the Crossrail excavations. What's more, it can move 16 million tonnes of sewage annually and goes underwater through East London. Thus, with this article on London's deepest sewer, we end this article on a very low note.

A HISTORY OF CROSSRAIL AND THE ELIZABETH LINE

The United Kingdom's great new engineering marvel, a seventy-three-mile railway dubbed the Elizabeth Line, opened in 2022 and runs through Berkshire, Buckinghamshire, Essex, and London. It is the longest commuter rail in the country and is able to bring in more people to London at speeds approximating 90 mph. Of course, all of us are just a little bit excited about this and want to share with you everything we've gleaned about the project since its announcement. We will walk you through the fascinating (and surprisingly long) history of Crossrail, the construction challenges, how it works, and how to use it.

HISTORY

You might be amazed to discover that the roots of Crossrail don't go back just a couple of decades, but well over a century. The scheme was first thought up in the 1880s, but ultimately nothing was done about it even as stations were constructed in London. The idea wouldn't come up again until

1943 and even though World War II was not yet over, planners for the city were already thinking about what would become of London after the war. It was part of Patrick Abercrombie's County of London Plan released that year and his Greater London Plan published in 1944.

The Railway Committee that was part of the London Plan then formed in 1944 and reported in both 1946 and 1948. The committee devised several routes labeled "A" through "F", but only ended up giving the go-ahead for route "C" that eventually became the Victoria line. However, while the original scheme proposed larger tunnels, the Victoria line was built with smaller-diameter Underground lines. The idea of larger Tube lines was largely forgotten about while London had other issues on its plate. Ultimately, however, while Abercrombie's early Crossrail-type proposal did not go through, other ideas such as London's "Green Belt" and "New Towns" for displaced Londoners were adopted.

Crossrail would not pick up steam again until 1974 when the Greater London Council and Department of the Environment published the London Rail Study. This was the birth of the modern scheme for Crossrail, and the report even gave the new line its name. The point of the report was to estimate London's future transport needs and proposed two tunnels: a northern tunnel that would join British Rail's Western Region lines before Paddington to the Eastern Region lines past Bethnal Green. The London Rail Study report was the first to actually propose a concrete scheme that was more than just another Tube line, but a mainline railway that went underground. However, the £300 million price tag was just a little more than London could afford at the time.

The Central London Rail Study of 1989 picked up where 1974 left off, proposing "East-West Crossrail", "City Crossrail," and "North-South Crossrail" schemes. The "East-West Crossrail" scheme won out in 1990, but a private bill submitted to Parliament in 1991 had an overall cost of £2 billion in 1993 money and the Private Bill Committee rejected it in 1994. The committee felt that a case "had not been made" for the Crossrail scheme, but even though it didn't approve Crossrail at that time, it still put in place "Safeguarding Directions" under the Transport and Works Act system to keep development in London from interfering with the scheme.

Seven years later, Transport for London and the Department for Transport would form the Cross London Rail Links venture to promote Crossrail. This joint-venture then made over fifty presentations in thirty different locations over 2003 and 2004 to explain the plans and enlist public support. The Crossrail Bill was then introduced into Parliament in 2005 and Transportation Secretary Ruth Kelly issued new safeguarding directions to protect the proposed routes of the final Crossrail scheme. The bill then went to the House of Lords in February 2008 and was amended before receiving Royal Assent in July and officially became the Crossrail Act 2008. At the time it was approved, the final cost was estimated at £15.9 billion. Of course, now that the scheme was approved and the funding secured from TfL, DfT, Network Rail, BAA (now Heathrow Airport Holdings), and the City of London, the real fun could begin.

CONSTRUCTION

The work to build this massive transportation project began on May 15, 2009, when construction crews started to do the deep foundation work at what would become the future Canary Wharf station. Other stations soon followed, including Tottenham Court Road, Farringdon, and Paddington in 2010, then Whitechapel, Woolwich, Bond Street, and Liverpool Street in 2011, and more from 2012 through 2013. Ultimately, construction added ten new stations while another thirty-one stations would be upgraded as part of the line and connect to the twenty-six miles of tunnels.

And speaking of tunnels, those twenty-six miles were dug by some of the most marvelous machines on the planet. The TBMs (or tunnel boring machines) were essentially drilling rigs on wheels, each with a diameter of twenty-three, as long as fourteen London busses end-to-end, and weighing as much as 143 of those busses. A total of eight custom machines were made just for this project and they worked twenty-four hours a day, seven days a week across ten different tunneling sections of thirteen miles from May 2012 to May 2015. Each tunneling machine had a name and it was TBM Victoria that made the final push into Farringdon to complete the tunneling part of the construction.

Of course, when you're tunneling out that much dirt, there are several concerns to address. Before the tunneling even started, core samples had to be taken along the proposed routes. These samples turned up approximately five layers of geological activity that helped to tell a lot about the very ground under Londoners' feet. From the surface to the base, these layers included terrace gravels, London clay (a dense clay that formed from the sea that once covered much of southeast England), Lambeth group (a geological stratum that is composed of gravels, sands, silts, and clays about 55 million years ago, Thanet sands (close to 60 million years old), and chalk (70-80 million years old). During both the construction of the stations and the tunnels, it was important to construct vertical shafts and horizontal pipes radiating from those shafts in order to keep the ground stable. Once tunneling was completed, the shafts were refilled.

Another issue that inevitably came up during filming was the uncovering of artifacts. In a city of so much history, where humans had lived as far back as 900,000 years ago, the Crossrail team knew it had an extraordinary opportunity to uncover more of London's story. Since construction began, a team of over 100 archaeologists worked with digging teams to recover tens of thousands of items from over forty excavation sites. These efforts culminated in an exhibition at the Museum of London Docklands in 2017 of 500 of the most fascinating objects that archaeologists uncovered from early-20th Century jam jars to 8,000-year-old flint tools. Ultimately, the exhibition was a huge success, drawing in 96,750 visitors while it was open.

And if you're wondering what happened to all that dirt

dug up during construction, it certainly got put to good use. Roughly ninety-eight percent of the excavated earth was reused, with three million tons helping to create a wetland nature reserve on Wallasea Island that is twice the size of the City of London. Additionally, the dirty found homes in landfills restored to become commercial parks and green spaces, other nature preserves, golf courses, and even grazing pasture for livestock.

The process of constructing the stations, network rail works, railway systems, and the train and railway depots. The final stages of construction began in 2017, with the final pieces of track being laid out in July. The tracks included standard track slabs and direct fixed track as well as high attenuation sleepers, floating track slab light, and floating track slab heavy to reduce noise and vibrations in places such as Soho and the Barbican. Thirty-three miles of rail were installed along with 63,000 sleepers and over 13,500 cubic meters of concrete was poured along the tracks. For the station tunnels, crews used sprayed concrete that enables huge underground spaces and curved walls.

Then is when the major delays set in. A combination of factors led to an almost 5-year delay in the opening of the line. It took longer to integrate the signaling systems than they anticipated. It turns out, getting a state-of-the-art railway to work with Victorian engineering is a challenge! Some of the stations, like Bond Street, took way longer to fit out than they had planned. Costs spiraled out of control. It was set to be a major disaster.

And then there was a REAL disaster.

COVID struck in 2020, and that forced construction to grind to a halt for months until it could resume safely with new COVID protocols. This made things take even longer, and cost even more. But finally, in spring 2022, part of the network was ready to open, and then in Autumn 2022, the line was fully integrated and opened completely. You can now go from Heathrow through central London super-fast.

The line also got a new name - while the company building the line continued to be called Crossrail, the line itself is now called the Elizabeth Line, named in honor of Queen Elizabeth II. She was able to open the line in person in May 2022, one of her last major public events before her death.

HOW IT WORKS

At this point, unless you were already familiar with Crossrail, you may be thinking "What's the big deal? It's just another Underground train, isn't it?" Wrong. Crossrail trains are more than just new Tube trains. The fleet that supports London's new transport route was purpose-built with an aim towards being both energy-efficient and high-performance. For that reason, the rolling stock (a term for vehicles that move on a railway) was developed to be so efficient that a train should be able to roll into the station every two minutes. The trains actually generate electricity as they travel along the track that goes back into its own systems, resulting in thirty-percent less energy usage while greatly increasing travel time.

TfL already started putting these trains into service in June 2017 between Liverpool Street and Shenfield, and by the time they transfer over to Crossrail, they'll join a fleet seventy strong by December 2019, each train 200 meters long and able to transport 1500 passengers at a time. The large, clear areas around the doors are meant to help passengers embark and disembark with greater ease and each carriage has four dedicated wheelchair spots to assist passengers with disabilities. And, as an extra perk, platforms and trains both will be equipped with 4G wi-fi so passengers never lose a data signal on their journey.

Speaking of signaling, Crossrail will use a system developed by Siemans PLC and Invensys Rail Limited. Crossrail actually uses two distinct signaling systems, one for the outer branches and another for the Crossrail Tunnel itself. The outer branches utilize the European Train Control System that is uniform in Europe and assists with interoperability, such as when trains from France travel into Germany and vice-versa. While in the Crossrail Tunnel, trains will operate on Communication-Based Train Control, which is normal for most underground metro systems. The trains will change over from one to the other on an open piece of track prior to and immediately after exiting the tunnel.

HOW TO USE IT

And we get to the final, all-important question—how do I use Crossrail? Previously, TfL announced that fares to use the Elizabeth line would be pay-as-you-go similar to the Underground and the Oyster system, making the cost no less expensive. Thus, peak fares Whitechapel to Paddington are £2.90, Canary Wharf to Haynes & Harrington fares are £4.70, and Bond Street to Oxford Circus are £2.40 anytime. You can also still use single fares from station to station as normal. Of course, the fares being the same also means that capping limits on Oyster and contactless cards, so there is a slight drawback.

What's more, as of May 2018, you can now use the Oyster card on TfL to get to Heathrow, and once the Elizabeth line is fully open, the service will pass to Crossrail, and use of the Oyster card will still be possible. Interestingly enough, even once Crossrail service is fully open to Heathrow, the Heathrow Express between the airport and Paddington station will continue to operate—though that will still not let you use the Oyster card. For further questions about cost and journey time, Crossrail already has its Journey Time Calculator up and running on its website.

In the end, London and the surrounding counties are going to be getting quite a lot in exchange for the £20+ billion spent on Crossrail. The line is already projected to bring another £42 billion to the country's economy. If you're heading from Shenfield to Heathrow Terminal 4, the total journey will take roughly 83 minutes instead of over two hours using the current transportation network. An estimated 200 million users will take advantage of the new Crossrail system, being able to move through London at an unprecedented rate and ushering in a new era for British transport. The Elizabeth Line will now fade into the background of London life like it has always been there. And arguments begin over the future

TRIVIA

TEN INTERESTING FACTS ABOUT THE METROPOLITAN

The Metropolitan Line (or "Met" as it's known) is the oldest line on the London Underground. It was founded in 1863 as the Metropolitan Railway and ran from Paddington to Farrington Street, mostly running goods as well as people. It expanded further shortly after it opened and today runs from Aldgate all the way out to Hertfordshire and Buckinghamshire. In all that time, the Metropolitan Line has developed quite a number of interesting facts that we have to share with you. Join us as we delve into the Met's history and relate some of its more fascinating stories.

THE FIRST

As mentioned above, the Met was the first Underground Line, but that's not the whole of it. In fact, the Metropolitan Line was the first of its kind anywhere in the world. It was the idea of Charles Pearson, Solicitor to the City, who had been campaigning for it since 1830 and wrote a pamphlet to promote it as a way to ease congestion in 1845. Pearson's original idea was for the trains to be pushed by air, which was quite different from the steam-powered locomotives that ultimately powered the Met's first cars. The Underground will still use steam-powered trains for special events.

KIND OF A BIG DEAL

When the Met launched on January 10, 1863, it was extremely popular. The first day it ran saw some 30,000 passengers.

MERGER

The Metropolitan Railway only ran for seventy years before it merged with the United Electric Railways Company of London (owners of the Piccadilly Line, Bakerloo Line, Central London Railway, and more) along with numerous bus operators and tramway companies to form the London Passenger Transport Board (a precursor to Transport for London) in 1933.

SPEED

Trains running on the Metropolitan Line can reach speeds of up to 60 miles per hour.

SOMEWHERE OUT THERE

The Metropolitan Line runs the furthest out of London of any of the Underground's lines. Its furthest station is Chesham, twenty-five miles outside of the city. The longest distance between Chesham and another station is 3.89 miles, which is the Chalfont & Latimer station.

THIRD PLACE

The Met is the third-longest of the Underground's routes at 67 kilometers (42 miles). It is only outdone by the Piccadilly Line at 71 kilometers and the Central Line at 74 kilometers. When it comes to number of stations, the Metropolitan Line is actually 6th. The lines with the most stations are District (60), Piccadilly (53), Northern (50), Central (49), and Circle (36).

ANOTHER FIRST

While it seems like this should have happened much sooner, the Metropolitan Line became the first to have an air-conditioned, walkthrough train in 2010.

ELEMENTARY

When the Metropolitan Line opened in 1863, Baker Street was one of its first stations. It expanded further in 1868 with new platforms and added other lines later on. In a nod to Baker Street's most famous fictional resident, the tilework features a silhouette of Sherlock Holmes. At one point, Platform 2 also featured a nod to his infamous rival with a pub named Moriarty.

FAMOUS FORMER LANDOWNER

Of course, Baker Street isn't the only station with some literary connection. Barbican station actually sits on land that was once owned by William Shakespeare. Barbican station opened only two years after the Met began, and at that point, it was known as Aldersgate Street, then Aldersgate in 1910, Aldersgate & Barbican in 1924, and finally, just Barbican in 1968.

BEDLAM & PLAGUE

Liverpool Street station was built over the site of the infamous Bethlehem Hospital, a mental institution that coined the word "Bedlam." In 2015, thousands of skeletons were found during the construction of the Elizabeth line, the remnants of a burial pit created for victims of the Black Death.

TEN INTERESTING FACTS AND FIGURES ABOUT THE VICTORIA LINE

Named for one of the greatest monarchs in British history, the Victoria line is one of the newer additions to the London Underground, if newer can be said to include a line that opened over fifty years ago. Of course, saying that it's named for Queen Victoria could also be a stretch, since originally the line ran from Victoria station to Walthamstow. Of course, even though it's a teenager compared to some of the older lines in the Underground, the Victoria Line still has plenty of interesting facts about it, which we have laid out below.

WHOLE LOTTA DIRT

During construction of the Victoria Line, construction workers excavated one million tonnes of earth.

SHOCKING DISCOVERIES

Doing any kind of construction work in a city as old as London is bound to turn up the odd find every so often. While digging up all that dirt for the tunnels, the workers managed to uncover fossils of marine mollusks and human remains from a plague pit.

WHAT'S IN A NAME

As mentioned, the Victoria Line is actually named for Victoria station which was once a terminus, and the station was named for Queen Victoria. Other names proposed included the portmanteau "Walvic Line" for its original termini, "Viking Line" (Victoria and King's Cross), Mayfair Line, and the West End Line. During its planning stages, the line was simply called "Route C".

MOO MOO CHOO CHOO

When there was a creamery at Vauxhall, "milk trains" used to run through the line, stopping at Vauxhall to fill up from a special tube that ran from the creamery before continuing on.

PRETTY SHORT

At 13.25 miles of track, the Victoria Line is actually the second shortest route in the Underground, with the shortest being the Waterloo and City Line, which is 1.47 miles and only has two stations. Like the Waterloo and City Line, the Victoria Line is the only other line that remains entirely underground.

STAYS BUSY THOUGH

Despite being the second shortest line on the Tube, the Victoria Line is by no means deserted. In fact, with 36 trains per hour and 250 million passengers per year, the Victoria Line is actually the most frequently used train service in the United Kingdom and the second-most traveled line in the world. The Victoria Line is also home to the busiest Underground station in Oxford Circus, which sees 98 million passengers annually.

GROWING

While the initial route ran from Victoria to Walthamstow when the Victoria Line opened in 1968, the line's first expansion came in 1971 when the Brixton station opened and Pimlico station followed in 1972.

AN AUSPICIOUS OPENING DAY

When the Victoria Line began service on September 1, 1968, it made history in a number of ways. For one, it was the first Underground line running across London to have been constructed since 1907. Second, and more importantly, the official opening on March 7, 1969, marked the first time the monarch had ever been on the Tube when Queen Elizabeth II rode on it.

BEAUTIFUL TILEWORK

One of the most striking parts of the Victoria Line is the tilework in each station. As the line was constructed, it was decided that each would have its own tilework to identify it. Finsbury Park Station, for example, displays a pair of dueling pistols for when men used to duel one another in the park after hours. Each tilework in the seat recesses relates to the station's name, so see if you can guess how each one is tied to its name.

UNDERGROUND MICE

It's believed that half a million mice live in the Underground. It's not hard to imagine, then that the two battling over a crumb in Sam Rowley's award-winning photo "Station Squabble" could have been in a station along the Victorian Line. The photo won the Wildlife Photographer of the Year Linux People Choice Award for 2019 from the Natural History Museum in London.

TEN INTERESTING FACTS ABOUT THE PICCADILLY LINE

The Piccadilly Line is one of the most popular in London, owing largely to the fact that most of the city's greatest monuments fall along its route, including the British Museum, Hyde Park, and Buckingham Palace. Running from Cockfosters, it spits towards its western terminus, with one line going to Uxbridge and the other to Heathrow Airport, which helps to make it the fourth-busiest line in the Underground. Since its opening as the Great Northern, Piccadilly, and Brompton Railway, the Piccadilly Line has racked up a number of interesting facts, and we have ten of the best for you.

DEFINITELY NOT AN EXPRESS TRAIN

If you're looking to get somewhere fast, you might want to take the Metropolitan line that shares some of the Piccadilly's stations. Otherwise, you might find yourself hitting a lot of stops as the Piccadilly Line's 53 stations are the most of any Underground route.

IT'S A FIRST

Between 1975 and 1977, the Underground worked to extend the Piccadilly Line out to Heathrow Airport. In doing so, the Underground became the first subway in the world to link to an airport. The Underground further expanded its connection to Heathrow by adding a station at Terminal 4 in 1986 and Terminal 5 in 2008.

CATCHING A FLIGHT

And speaking of Heathrow, the earliest trains out to the station leave at 4:45 AM, so you're in luck if you have an early flight. The final stop for the Piccadilly Line is Rayners Lane at 1:19 AM for those who stuck around until last call.

YOU COULD WALK THAT

The shortest distance between two stations is the one between Covent Garden and Leicester Square, which is only a mere 300 meters (984 feet). It takes about twenty seconds to travel between the stations and in 2017, the trip cost £4.90.

PETITIONS DO WORK

At least, they did in 1923. Originally, the Piccadilly Line ran from Finsbury Park to Hammersmith. That wasn't enough for the people of London, however, and in 1923 they amassed roughly 30,000 signatures to get the line extended on a petition that was delivered to the Ministry of Transport.

WHAT'S IN A NAME?

Piccadilly may sound like an unusual name, but it's one with an interesting history. Derived from Piccadilly Circus that the line passes through, the origin of Piccadilly comes from the 17th Century frilled collars called "piccadils." These collars were made by a tailor named Roger Baker, who became rich from making them.

SECRET TUNNEL! SECRET TUNNEL!

The Earl's Court Underground Station has a corridor and some escalators that have been long abandoned. The corridor ran between the station and the exhibition center but has gone disused since the exhibition center closed in 2014.

WAR CONTRIBUTIONS

During World War II, the Aldwych branch's Eastern Line was used to house the treasures of the British Museum to keep them safe from bombing, while the Western tunnel served as an air-raid shelter. Additionally, the now-disused Brompton Road station served as a control room for anti-aircraft guns.

HISTORICAL SIGNIFICANCE

There are four stations on the Piccadilly Line that are Grade II listed: Oakwood, Southgate, Arnos Grove, and Sudbury Town. This is twice as many as any other Tube line. All of them except for Sudbury Town are part of the Cockfosters branch.

A BIT OF AN UPGRADE

Between 2014-2015, the Piccadilly Line was supposed to get new trains and new signaling which would increase its efficiency by twenty-four percent. Bids were submitted in 2008, but the order was canceled in 2010. Currently, the Piccadilly Line runs an "obsolete" signaling system that's been in place since the 1950s. Instead, the line was given a temporary upgrade, and it's finally due for the real upgrade to the trains and the signaling in 2023.

TEN INTERESTING FACTS ABOUT THE NORTHERN LINE

Running from Southwest London to Northwest London on a crescent-shaped path, the Northern Line has an interesting history that separates it from the other Underground routes. Whereas most of the other original lines that made up the London Underground were formed out of complete, pre-existing railways when they merged as part of the London Transport Safety Board, the Northern Line was a merger of the City & South London Railway and the Charing Cross, Euston & Hampstead Railway. The line has expanded greatly since, extending to Morden in the south and separating into three separate branches to the north. As with many of London's Underground routes, it holds a lot of interesting facts and we've identified some of our favorites below.

DO YOU KNOW WHO YOU SOUND LIKE?

Word has it that Paul McCartney and Sting have both performed as buskers (or street performers) on the Northern Line while disguised.

LONG TUNNEL IS LOOOOOOONG

The Northern Line is home to the Underground's longest tunnel, running from East Finchley to Morden for 17.3 miles.

THE HIGHS AND THE LOWS

The line has the deepest station with Hampstead being 192 feet underground as well as the highest elevation, rising 60 feet above the street as the line goes over the Dollis Brook viaduct over Dollis Road.

UNFINISHED BUSINESS

The Northern Line has disused stations, but also one that was never completed. The North End Station between Hampstead and Golders Green was started in 1903, but construction was halted for a housing development that was ultimately never constructed. By the time construction had stopped in 1906, much of the tunnels, the passageways, and the lift shafts had been dug. Even unfinished, it still managed to serve a purpose as a storage site during World War II and as part of London's civil defense during the Cold War.

MIND THE GAP

The iconic phrase was first recorded by sound engineer Peter Lodge in 1968 after the actor hired for the job demanded royalties. While several other voice actors and personalities have recorded the words that play throughout the Tube system, Embankment Station still features Lodge after his widow asked them to keep it so she could still hear his voice.

PEAK HOURS

The Northern Line splits off when it gets to Central London

starting after Kennington and coming back together at Euston. Running through a number of the city's popular stations including Leicester Square, Embankment, Waterloo, Charing Cross, and London Bridge, it's no surprise that the Northern Line commands the greatest number of trains during peak service at 91.

GROWING AND GROWING

As one of the busiest lines in the Underground, the Northern Line has expanded several times as the city grew in the 20th Century. When the line opened in 1890, it ran from Stockwell to King William Street (the latter now a disused station). After about ten years, the line was expanded to have it run to Moorgate via Bank Station and extended further to Clapham Common and Euston Station in 1907.

HOW LONG CAN YOU HOLD YOUR BREATH?

While the air quality of the London Underground has improved since the start of the millennium, a 2002 study discovered that the air was 73-times worse in the Underground tunnels than it was on the street. That same study stated that twenty minutes on the Northern Line was the equivalent to smoking a cigarette.

BETTER HOPE THIS ESCALATOR NEVER BREAKS

Normally that prospect isn't so bad, since as comedian Mitch Hedberg stated: "Escalators can never break, they can only become stairs." However, that becomes a little more daunting when you realize the escalator at Angel station in Islington is 197 feet long.

FINAL THOUGHTS

The first baby born on the London Underground was Marie

TEN INTERESTING FACTS AND FIGURES ABOUT THE LONDON OVERGROUND

A complement to the London Underground (and not a 'Tube' line but an important rail network in London), the London Overground is the Tube's lesser-known cousin, a network of commuter trains that rely on above-ground tracks. This is similar to the group of private-owned organizations that make up National Rail, though the Overground is a public service owned by Transport for London and is exclusive to the city. Today, the London Overground involves six routes that provide a ring around the city as well as transport into Central London and the suburbs. To help better familiarize you with the Overground, we've laid out ten interesting facts about it below.

A RAIL TIME CAPSULE

The Peckham Rye Overground station is one of the jewels of the service. The Old Waiting Room there is an amazing example of Victorian design and was considered one of the most beautiful station waiting rooms in South London. It opened in 1865 and is Grade II listed; however, it was bricked off for over fifty years before reopening in 2017 for limited engagements.

THE ONLY ONE

Of all the Overground stations, Rotherhithe is the sole station with escalators.

GROWING OVER TIME

The Overground opened in 2007, and the line originally ran from Watford Junction in the north to Clapham Junction in the south, as well as Richmond in the west and Barking in the East. Phase I extension finished in 2010, expanding south from Dalston to West Croydon. The Overground added the South London in 2012 which includes stations at the aforementioned Peckham Rye, Denmark Hill, Clapham High Street, and more. Service was again extended in 2015 to stations on Liverpool Street, and TfL has plans to add even more branches by 2026.

TRAVELING OLD ROUTES

Specifically, the southern extension of the East London line follows the old Croydon Canal route from the West Croydon station to the New Cross station. This route used to be a waterway passage for boats pulled by horses and closed in 1836.

IT'S ELECTRIC! BOOGIEWOOGIEWOOGIE!

The trains are anyway. Electric Class 710 trains were added to the London Overground's lines in January 2018 and replaced old diesel Class 172s. The trains are updated with USB ports for charging devices and real-time information screens. Plus, they can carry twice the number of passengers than the older models, somewhere around 700 riders.

GONE BUT NOT FORGOTTEN

Performance venue Village Underground was built under the former site of the Broad Street Rail Viaduct, which is located near the Shoreditch High Street station. Remnants of the building's past can be seen with the old trains perched on the roof.

ARCH-BUSINESSES

In London, real estate is at a premium, so plenty of shops, galleries, restaurants, and more set themselves up in the arches under the various Overground lines. Amongst the quirkier businesses found under these archways include: London Community Boxing in Peckham, the winery London Renegade Wine, Institute of Light cinema, art gallery/wrestling venue Resistance Gallery, and board game café Draughts, amongst others. It's worth exploring the archways to see what other odd and wonderful places you can find.

UTILIZING SPACE

And speaking of premium real estate, even unused portions of the Overground can find a new purpose. The East Curve Garden in Dalston is one such example. It was planned as a rail line to link the East Dalston Junction Station to the good yards and the North London Line, and you can still see the curve on aerial photos.

THE GINGER LINE

A nickname for the Overground due to its orange hue, the color was inherited from the East London line that became the Overground when it was transferred from the Underground. The orange has its own unique shade (Pantone 158C). The color is also used for all the Overground's lines, unlike the Underground, that uses different colors for each. Additionally, like the Docklands Light Railway, the Overground uses a double line instead of a solid line to distinguish itself from the Tube.

SECRET STATION

One of the Overground's stations doesn't actually appear on the map. Battersea Park station is a skeleton station that only runs two trains at 6 AM and 11 PM going to Clapham High Street.

10 INTERESTING FACTS ABOUT THE JUBILEE LINE

The newest line of the London underground isn't exactly young anymore. Added to the network in 1979, some of the tracks go back as far as 1932 and the stations to 1879. Today, it runs in a diagonal pattern from Stanmore in Northwest London and curving up at the end to Stratford in East London. Of course, being the youngest of the Underground lines doesn't mean that there is any shortage of interesting facts about the Jubilee Line. From royal connections to interesting safety features, there are plenty of fascinating tidbits.

THE ROYAL LINE

The Jubilee Line was original to be named the Fleet Line after the River Fleet that runs through the city. However, when London Transport sought to introduce the Silver Jubilee bus line in 1975 in anticipation of the 25th Anniversary of Queen Elizabeth II's reign, a name change was deemed to be in order, and the Fleet Line became the Jubilee Line. The line is denoted with the color silver on the Underground map as a reference to the Silver Jubilee, and the official color is Pantone 430. Prince Charles opened it officially on 30 April 1979.

THERE'S JUST NO PLEASING SOME PEOPLE

A 2012 survey showed that the Jubilee Line was the most complained about of all the Underground lines. In one month, the Jubilee Line received 331 complaints, while second place went to the Victoria Line at 317.

HEALTH & SAFETY

Unfortunately, one of the more popular methods of suicide in London is to jump in front of an oncoming Tube train. To safeguard against this, the eastern extension of the Jubilee Line has automatic glass screens that are designed to discourage potential jumpers, only opening once the train arrives at the station.

MAKING CONNECTIONS

The Jubilee Line is the only one in the Underground system that connects with all of the other lines.

THE SILVER SCREEN

Along with the disused Aldwych Station on the Piccadilly Line, the non-operational Jubilee Line complex at Charing Cross Station sees its fair share of filming for television and movie productions. The complex tends to be used when production crews need a more modern-looking Underground station and has been seen in the television program Spooks as well as films such as 28 Weeks Later and Skyfall. This year, the station doubled as a pop-up cinema showing such films as Blade Runner, Strangers on a Train, An American Werewolf in London, and Paddington.

WE HAVE TO GO DEEPER

The Jubilee Line is the deepest of all the lines at 105 feet (32 meters) below sea level, which is 221 feet (68.8 meters) below ground level.

MAGICAL ARTWORK

The blue cone wall in Southwark Station is said to have been inspired by a set piece from an 1816 production of The Magic Flute. Meanwhile, the modern look of the Canary Wharf Station was designed by Sir Norman Foster, who also designed 30 St. Mary Axe, better known as the Gherkin. It opened in 1999, and a 2013 poll declared it as the "most beloved" station on the Underground.

SO CLOSE, BUT SO FAR

The two closest stations on the Jubilee Line are Waterloo and Southwark, which are less than half a mile from each other. Walking from one to the other takes roughly half as long. The two furthest stations are Kingsbury and Wembley Park.

TRAIN NUMBERS

Jubilee Line trains run 29,208 kilometers on an average weekday, 27,000 km on Saturday, and 21,000 km on Sundays. The trains used to have only six carriages but later added a seventh, meaning they can carry 6,000 more passengers per day. Each one of the carriages can seat 234 people and are 126 meters long.

WORN OUT

The rail track on the Jubilee Line extension is topped with aluminum, which is softer than the wheels of the train. This means that the metal wears out faster, but the tracks are easier and more cost-effective to replace.

TEN INTERESTING FACTS AND FIGURES ABOUT DOCKLANDS LIGHT RAILWAY

Like a little brother to the London Underground, the Docklands Light Rail transportation system was developed following the revitalization of the Docklands in East London. The DLR as it's known opened in 1987 serving much of Eastern London like its own little Underground. While still under Transport for London, it's run as a separate light metro rail service, though it does connect to the Tube as well. If you ever wanted to know more about the Tube's little brother, we've got some interesting facts for you to ponder over while you ride.

SOME NUMBERS

First things first. While the DLR may seem pretty small compared to the Tube, it's just as big as any line. It has a total of 45 stations and its lines stretch out over two tracks for roughly 24 miles. It also has an estimated daily ridership of 340,000 people.

ALL THE TRANSPORTATION

DLR perhaps connects to more varied transportation systems than any other part of London. Besides the Underground, it also connects to the Emirates Cable Car system that crosses over the Thames.

UNDER THE RIVER

Besides the Emirates Cable Car, the Docklands Light Railway actually goes under the Thames at two points: Canary Wharf and Woolwich.

GROWING AND GROWING

When DLR opened in 1987, it had only 15 stations along its two tracks. The first expansion came in 1991 when it opened Bank station. Several more expansions have been made from 1991 to 1994, 1996 to 1999, 2004 to 2009, and as recently as 2011. Branches stretch out to Lewisham in the south, Stratford and Stratford International in the north, Beckton and Woolwich Arsenal in the east, and Bank and Tower Gateway to the west into Central London.

2012 OLYMPICS

DLR's ability to transport people across London was keenly felt during the 2012 Summer Olympics and Paralympics. DLR ran all the way out to Olympic Park as well as venues in Greenwich, Central London, and the Royal Docks. The Docklands Light Railway saw double its usual daily passengers during the games and causing it to hit over 100 million passengers for 2012/2013.

CATCHING A FLIGHT

The DLR sports the only other line that connects to an airport in London. The first is the Underground's Piccadilly Line which connects to Heathrow. DLR connects to the London City Airport.

WHERE ARE THE PEOPLE?

While there are certainly plenty of passengers even when there isn't a major event in London, you'll notice something keenly missing—drivers. The trains are controlled by a computer and fully automated and thus don't have a driver's cabin. In case of an emergency, however, a Passenger Service Assistant is on the train that can access a panel at either end to take control as necessary. Even the stations have minimal staff, with the DLR's underground stations having more personnel to meet fire and safety requirements.

DEEP DOWN

Only five of DLR's stations are underground: Woolwich Arsenal, Island Gardens, Stratford International, Cutty Sark, and Bank. Of these, Bank is the deepest underground at 41.4 meters below the surface.

NO, THE OTHER ONE

DLR has one station called Abbey Road, but it's not connected to the Beatles in any way. There are actually two Abbey Roads in London, one in the City of Westminster and the other in West Ham. It's the former that's where you'll find Abbey Road Studios and the famous zebra crossing. Those heading to the DLR station to find that spot will be sorely disappointed.

THE CITY'S FAVORITE

In a 2017 YouGov poll, the DLR was a joint favorite transport line of Londoners, tied with the Jubilee Line of the London Underground.

TOP 13 FACTS ABOUT THE TUBE

Recently the iconic London Underground Celebrated its 150th anniversary. To celebrate the birthday of this London institution, here are 13 facts and figures about it!

1. Today, the Tube carries 1,107 million passengers each year to 270 stations.

2. London Underground is colloquially known as 'the Tube', which originally referred to the deep-level train lines which were used by trains of a smaller and more circular cross-section, as opposed to the less deep "cut-and-cover" lines that were built first and originally used steam locomotives. The term now embraces the whole system.

3. The average speed of a Tube train is 33km per hour/ 20.5 mph

4. The number of miles/km traveled by each Tube train each year is 114,500 miles/184,269km

5. The length of the Tube network is 402km/249 miles

6. Every day over 1000 people accidentally leave something on the Tube. All the items are sent to a basement office in Baker Street that employs 40 full-time staff. At any one time it holds 200,000 items of lost property; some of the weirder items in the past have included Samurai swords, false teeth, three dead bats, and a 14-foot boat. Items not claimed after 3 months are either sold at auction or given to charity.

7. The disused tube station Aldwych is often seen on screen, and was used as a location for scenes in Superman IV: The Quest for Peace, Atonement and V for Vendetta

8. The maximum depth of the Tube below ground level is at Holly Bush Hill in Hampstead, where the deep-level lines run 68.8 m/221ft under ground

9. The longest escalator is at Angel station: it's 60m/197ft, with a vertical rise of 27.5m/90ft

10. Baker Street is the station with the most platforms – it has 10

11. London's busiest Tube station is Waterloo, with 57,000 people entering during the three-hour morning peak. The busiest station in terms of passengers each year is also Waterloo with 82 million

12. During 2011-12 The London Underground carried a record number of passengers with 1.171 billion journeys made

13. Albus Dumbledore, a character from the Harry Potter series, has a scar just above his left knee in the shape of the Tube map

TEN INTERESTING FACTS ABOUT THE CENTRAL LINE

The red line on the London Underground map represents the Central Line, a fixture of the Tube since it opened as the Central London Railways in 1900. Today, it runs along an east-west axis from West Ruislip all the way up to Epping in Essex. As with other lines on the London Underground, the Central Line is certainly full of its own interesting facts and figures. What you find on its tracks, in its cars, and at its stations may surprise you, and you just might realize there's more to the Central Line than your morning commute.

A LONG STRANGE TRIP

The Central Line is easily the longest route on the London Underground. From West Ruislip to Epping stations, the line length is 46 miles (76 kilometers), with the longest direct route between the two stations being almost 34 miles (59.4 kilometers). There are a total of 49 stations along the Central Line, with seven lines that have closed since it opened. What's more, in 2011/2012, approximately 260.916 million people traveled on the line.

OUTSIDE THE LINES

The Central Line is one of the only two Underground lines to actually go outside of the Greater London area. Epping and Loughton are the only Central Line stations that go outside of Greater London. The other line that goes outside Greater London is the Metropolitan.

ORIGIN OF THE NAME

"The Tube" as a nickname for the London Underground began with Central London Railway in the 1900s. Its two penny fare combined with the cylindrical shape of the lines gave it the nickname "The Two Penny Tube," later shortened to just "The Tube." The nickname was eventually used for the entire Underground.

TWISTING AND TURNING

If you've ever wondered why the Central Line tunnels seem to twist and turn more than other Underground lines, it's because the Central Line actually follows the street pattern of Medieval London.

ART IMITATING LIFE

One of the stations on the line possesses the same name as a well-known television program. Grange Hill is both a station between Hainault and Chigwell and also a drama program focusing on events at the fictional Grange Hill School. The program is one of the longest-running in BBC history and was broadcast for thirty years from 1978 to 2008.

REPURPOSED FOR WAR

While many Underground stations were repurposed during World War II as air raid shelters, approximately two miles of the Central Line were shut down and converted into an aircraft factory. Electronics manufacturer Plessey utilized the Central Line as a factory after its original location was bombed by the Luftwaffe. This fact remained an official secret until the 1980s.

FAMOUS PASSENGERS

When the Central Line first ran in 1900, amongst its VIP passengers were Mark Twain and the Prince of Wales, the future King Edward VII.

THE LIGHT OF DAY

The Central Line has the most stations without an above ground building. Of the Central Line's 49 stations, five of them have no surface building. These stations include: Notting Hill Gate, Bank, Bethnal Green, Chancery Lane, and Gants Hill.

LAST OF ITS KIND

For years, the Greenford Station on the Central Line was home to the Underground's last remaining wooden escalator. Wooden escalators were largely replaced after the King's Cross fire of 1987. Recently, the Greenford Station has been the focus of upgrading that will include step-free access, a wider staircase, and a radar key toilet. Sadly, these renovations mean that the Underground's last wooden staircase will be gone by the time work is finished this summer.

A MUSEUM PIECE FOR THE MUSEUM

One of the Central Line's closed stations was the British Museum Station. It opened in 1900, but was shut down in 1933 after the expansion of the nearby Holborn station made the museum's station obsolete.

TEN INTERESTING FACTS ABOUT THE ELIZABETH LINE

Crossrail! Aka The Elizabeth Line. The long sought-after solution to London's commuter congestion, London Crossrail is a railway line that is separate from the London Underground east-to-west from Shenfield to Reading. The earliest proposals date back to World War II, but it wouldn't be until 2005 that a bill passed Parliament that would form the basis for today's central London rail system. Construction began in 2009, and the entire route was finally in operation by Autumn 2022, years overdue. For your reading pleasure, here are ten interesting facts and figures about the latest addition to Transport for London.

UNCOVERING HISTORY

It's not unusual for development in London to come across a body or two, such as when digging up a car park uncovered King Richard III. In March 2013, workers digging the tunnels for Crossrail uncovered 13 skeletons under a road near Charterhouse Square, Farringdon. The bodies were believed to be plague victims from the 14th Century.

NEW STATIONS

The 10 new stations being constructed include: Tottenham

Court Road, Farringdon, Liverpool Street, White Chapel, Canary Wharf, Custom House, Paddington, Bond Street, Woolwich, and Abbey Wood.

A FEW NUMBERS

Crossrail is Europe's largest construction project, with 10,000 people working across 40 construction sites, including 10 new stations. 26 miles (42 km) of new tunnels are being built, and it's estimated the teams have created at least 100 meters of new tunnels per week. The government is eager for the results that Crossrail will bring, including giving 1.5 million people better access to central London, over 200 million users per year, and £42 billion to Britain's economy annually.

COST

The total projected cost of Crossrail is £14.8 billion (about $25 Billion USD). It ended up costing a lot more than that. Final numbers were not known at press time.

TUNNELING, TUNNELING

Eight tunneling machines have been used to carve out the 26 miles of tunnels for Crossrail. The last of these, named Elizabeth and Victoria, weigh 1,000 tonnes each, are 150 meters long, and have a diameter of 7 meters. For an idea of what the tunneling machines look like, they're similar to those seen in the American film Ocean's Thirteen.

AWARD-WINNING TUNNELING

Yes, there's actually an award show for tunneling known as the New Civil Engineer International Tunneling and Underground Space Awards. At the 2015 ceremony, the Bond Street station upgrade for the Underground won the Global Tunneling Project of the Year (Under $500 million) Award. Additionally,

Crossrail won awards for "Product/Equipment Innovation of the Year," "Rising Star of the Year," "Technical Innovation of the Year," "Rehabilitation Project of the Year," and "Tunnel Operator of the Year."

UNDERGROUND ARTIST

One of Crossrail's goals is to integrate arts, culture, and creativity into its construction project. As such, artist Julie Leonard has become the project's first "Artist in Residence" and has used her talents to depict the personalities and construction on the railway line. In addition to being an artist and printmaker, Leonard is also a digital artist and uses an app her mobile phone to create digital paintings of the ongoing construction.

WAIT FOR IT…

The first Crossrail service was expected to start in 2018. It did not open until May 2022.

MADE IN THE UK

95% of the contracts awarded for Crossrail have been to companies that are based within the United Kingdom. Of this percentage, 58% are small-to-medium sized companies that report their business has increased by 44% after they joined Crossrail. Crossrail is also expected to create 75,000 opportunities for businesses, including 55,000 full-time jobs.

PUTTING THE RUBBLE TO GOOD USE

Approximately 4.5 million tonnes of excavated material is going to be sent to Wallasea Island to create a new 1,500-acre nature reserve for the Royal Society for the Protection of Birds.

TEN INTERESTING FACTS ABOUT THE CENTRAL

Earning its name by running through Central London, the Central Line is one of the most important lines in the London Underground. The Central Line started as the Central London Railway in 1900 running east to west through the city. In 120 years of its existence, the Central Line has built up a very interesting history and some great facts to go with it. Combing through the miles of tunnels, we've found ten of the most interesting factoids about the Central Line that you ought to find fascinating.

DEEP UNDERGROUND

The Central Line has the most stations without a building above ground. These stations include Bank, Bethnal Green, Chancery Lane, Gants Hill, and Notting Hill Gate.

THE NUMBERS

It's not an exaggeration to say that the Central Line is one of the most important in the London Underground network.

It is the longest line in the Underground at 46 miles, which is just three miles short of the distance between Leeds and Manchester. The line also reported a total number of nearly 261 million passengers between 2016 and 2017.

I AIN'T 'FRAID OF NO GHOSTS

London is a city that has its share of specters and spirits, and that extends to the Underground as well. Liverpool Street Station was built over the site of the infamous Bethlehem Hospital, a mental institution that coined the word "Bedlam". In 2015, thousands of skeletons were found during the construction of the Crossrail line, the remnants of a burial pit created for victims of the Black Death. The former British Museum station is also believed to be haunted by the ghost of a mummy.

BUSIEST AND QUIETEST

The Central Line's busiest station is Oxford Circus, which saw nearly 85 million passengers during 2016 and 2017 due to its proximity to busy Oxford Street (the shipping district). By contrast, Roding sees maybe 250,000 passengers in a single year.

FORGOING TRAINS FOR PLANES

Prior to World War II, stations began an upgrade, lengthened to allow for eight-car trains. However, the war effort ceased the construction, and some new tenants moved into unused tunnels between Leytonstone and Newberry Park. The Pressley Company used the vacant tunnels as a factory to construct aircraft parts, employing some 2,000 people for the duration of the war.

NICKNAMES

Would you believe that the nickname "The Tube" didn't originate as a term for the whole of the Underground? It actually started as a nickname for the Central Line. Back when the line started in 1900, the line had a flat fare of two pennies, earning it the nickname "The Two-Penny Tube", which was later shortened to simply "The Tube".

EARLY ATTEMPTS AT CORPORATE SPONSORSHIPS?

In 1909, Harry Gordon Selfridge attempted to make a major push to have the Bond Street station name changed to "Selfridges" as a way to promote his store. Naturally, he was turned down. The store made another push in the 1930s to have its own subway connecting the station and the store but was refused yet again.

WHAT'S THAT SMELL?

In 2001, the Central Line attempted to freshen up its stations by pumping ascent known as "Madeline" through the vents. However, after a single day of use, the Underground canceled using the scent as passengers complained of feeling ill.

IS IT MADE OF...WOOD?

Greenford station was home to the Underground's last wooden escalator, which was removed in 2015. Most of the wooden escalators were removed after a fire at King's Cross station caused by a lit cigarette dropping into the escalator killed 31 people.

TRAIN JUMPERS

Suicides on the Central Line from people jumping in front of trains caused the Underground to install suicide pits beneath the tracks in 1926.

TEN INTERESTING FACTS ABOUT THE BAKERLOO LINE

If I had to pick a London Underground line with the most 'Londony' name, it would be the Bakerloo line (a portmanteau of Baker Street and Waterloo Railway). Here are a few interesting facts and figures about this famous Tube line.

THE BROWN LINE

Printed in brown on the Tube map, it serves 25 stations, 15 of which are underground, over 14.4 miles (23.2 km). It runs partly on the surface and partly in deep-level tube tunnels.

THE MIDDLE CHILD

This line opened well after the original tube lines, coming into service between 1906 and 1915. It was built following the plan for another railway line that was scrapped in the late 1800s.

DISTINCTIVE STATIONS

Since the line was most built at the same time, it has a unified design look, with most of the stations being designed by Leslie Green. The stations below ground use Art Nouveau decorative tiling by Leslie Green, and the above-ground stations are built in red brick with stone detailing in an Arts & Crafts style.

NOT SO BUSY

The Bakerloo line is the 9th busiest Tube line on the network and serves 111 million passengers annually.

OLD TRAINS

This line has the oldest rolling stock on the London Underground currently, which came into service in 1972. Due to funding issues, they're not likely to be replaced until the late 2030s or early 2040s - giving an incredibly long life to these trains!

SHERLOCK HOLMES CONNECTIONS

The line is named for Baker Street, but the station was already in existence when the line was built (it came into service in 1863). While Sherlock Holmes is a fictional character, there are many nods to the famous connection in the station - including themed tiles throughout the station.

ELECTRICITY.... REVERSED.

One oddity is that, almost from its opening until 1917, the Bakerloo operated with the polarity of the conductor rails reversed, the outside rail negative, and the center rail positive. This came about because the Bakerloo shared a power source with the District Railway. On the Bakerloo, the outside conductor rail tended to leak to the tunnel wall, whereas on the District Railway, the center rail shared a similar problem.

The solution was to reverse the polarity on the Bakerloo line, so that the negative rail leaked on both systems. In 1917, the two lines were separated when the LNWR began its New Line' service between Euston and Watford Junction, which the Bakerloo would share north of Queens Park.As a result, normal operation was restored.

SERVICE PATTERN

As of May 2021, weekday off-peak and Sunday services on Bakerloo line are:

4 tph (trains per hour) from Harrow & Wealdstone to Elephant & Castle
4 tph from Stonebridge Park to Elephant & Castle
8 tph from Queen's Park to Elephant & Castle
This forms a 16 tph service (or a train approximately every 4 minutes) between Queen's Park and Elephant & Castle. A 20 tph service runs on this section of the line during the weekday peak and all day on Saturdays.

OVER 100 YEARS

The line celebrated its centenary on 10 March 2006, when events were organized with actors and staff in Edwardian costumes to entertain travelers.

FIRE FIRE

In 2017, a big fire at Oxford Circus station caused disruption on the Bakerloo line. A number of people were treated for smoke inhalation after the fire broke out.

TEN INTERESTING FACTS ABOUT THE DISTRICT LINE

Running from the east in Upminster to Earl's Court in the west, the District Line forms one of the oldest London Underground lines in the service's history. The idea when the line began was that it would connect all of London's railway termini. Starting off as a separate underground railway, it was integrated with the other underground railways into the London Underground in 1933. Since that time, it has become the busiest of the Tube's sub-surface railways, and as you can imagine, this means that there are a lot of interesting facts for us to relate.

I'LL BE HOME FOR CHRISTMAS

The District Line first opened on Christmas Eve, 1868, just in time to get people back home for the holiday.

BUSY BUSY BUSY

As mentioned, the District Line is one of the busiest on the

London Underground. It is the fifth-busiest overall and the busiest of the sub-surface lines. In 2011/2012, it saw upwards of 208 million riders. It's not hard to understand why when you see that the District Line stretches for roughly 40 miles and has 60 stations, the most of any London Underground line.

BLOWN AWAY

On December 8, 1954, a tornado actually blew off the roof of the Gunnersbury station on the District Line. Six people were injured as a result.

SORRY FOR THE CONVENIENCE

The District Line was the first amongst the Tube lines to get an escalator, which was installed at the Earl's Court station in 1911. People weren't quite sure about this new-fangled invention, however, and the Tube reportedly hired a one-legged man to ride up and down the escalators to show people that they were safe.

ANOTHER FIRST

The Underground station of Stamford Brook on the District Line was the first to get an automatic ticket barrier installed in 1964.

IT'S NOT BIGGER ON THE INSIDE (WE THINK)

The Earl's Court station is also home to the last remaining functional Police Public Call Box in the city. Better known to modern people as the TARDIS (due to the original TARDIS taking on the look of a Police Box), it was saved from destruction by dedicated Doctor Who fans long after police boxes were no longer necessary. If you visit it in real life, you won't be able to get inside, but Google Earth offers a fun surprise to those who use their platform to enter it.

MISTER, CAN YOU SPARE A BONE?

Laddy, the Airedale Terrier, was a common fixture at Wimbledon station from 1949 to 1956. With a collection box strapped to his back, Laddie collected donations for the Southern Railway Servants Orphanage. After retirement, he went to live at the Southern Railway Home for Old People in Woking until his death in 1960. After that, he was stuffed and returned to Wimbledon station, where he was put on display and still collected money for charity until he was finally removed in 1990.

A RIVER RUNS THROUGH IT

During construction, the District Line encountered an issue in that the River Westbourne went right through the planned location of the Sloane Square Station. To get around this, the engineers essentially constructed a huge pipe through which the river could flow above the station. The District Line still runs under the River Westbourne, thanks to this piece of engineering.

END OF THE LINE

The District Line has been used twice to transport the remains of famous persons. The first was Prime Minister William Gladstone in 1898 from Westminster Station to his funeral at Westminster Abbey. The second was philanthropist Dr. Thomas Barnardo in 1905. He was the last dead body to be transported in this fashion.

IT'S NOT A PLATFORM; IT'S ART

Gloucester Road station has a disused Tube platform that's used for temporary art installations and can be rented out for special events.

TEN INTERESTING FACTS ABOUT THE WATERLOO AND

The shortest Tube Line, the Waterloo and City line connects just two stations, but provides a key traffic pattern for commuters to the City of London from London's suburbs in southwest London, Surrey, and Hampshire. Here are a few interesting facts about it.

THE SHORTEST

It's the shortest Tube line at just 1.47 miles or 2.37 kilometers.

THE DRAIN

Its nickname with locals is 'The Drain' because it's basically a pipe from Waterloo to The City.

TWO STATIONS

It has just two stations - London Waterloo and Bank, in the city of London (literally below the Bank of England).

DEPOT

Unlike the rest of the Tube network, its depot is located underground at Waterloo station. All maintenance is carried out underground.

NO SUNDAYS OR WEEKENDS

Because the focus of the line is commuters who work in the City of London, the trains usually do not run on weekends, except in limited circumstances - like for a special event.

IT'S FAST

The journey takes just 4 minutes. This is definitely the fastest end-to-end journey on the entire tube network!

YOU TUNNEL

Along your four-minute journey, you go under the Thames into the original Roman City of London.

RENOVATIONS ARE DISRUPTIVE

When the Tube stock needed to be updated, the entire line had to close for several months, and the old trains were lifted out of 'the drain' by crane and new ones lowered down, which was a slow and painstaking process.

PEOPLE, THE PEOPLE

Despite its short length and only having two stops, the line serves over 15 million passengers a year! Most are commuters who live outside of central London in the various southern home counties. Popular places to live if you work in the City of London.

FULLY ELECTRIC

When it was built in 1898, it was only the second electric underground railway and continues to run on DC power today.

10 INTERESTING FACTS ABOUT THE CIRCLE LINE

The Circle Line is one of London's oldest Tube Lines, but it also gets easily confused with the District Line, with which it shares a lot of track. But this unique line has long served central London and is a great way to get around for tourists. Here are a few interesting facts about the Circle Line.

NOT DEEP

The tunnels for the Circle line are not 'deep-level' tunnels like the Piccadilly or Bakerloo line, instead, they're sub-surface - built just below the surface using the 'cut and cover' method of construction. The road was dug up, the tunnels built, and then covered back over. You can hear the trains along the line as they're so close to the surface.

NO LONGER A CIRCLE

In 2009, the 'circle' was broken when the line was extended to run to Hammersmith using the Hammersmith & City route. Trains no longer run continuously around the circle, instead breaking the journey via different routes.

SEVEN CARS

In 2015, the six-car C Stock Trains were replaced with new S Stock trains that were seven cars in length. This allowed capacity to increase on the line.

ACTION STATIONS!

Printed in yellow on the Tube map, the 17-mile (27 km) line serves 36 stations, including most of London's main railway termini. Almost all of the route, and all the stations, are shared with one or more of the three other sub-surface lines, namely the District, Hammersmith & City, and Metropolitan lines.

MILLIONS AND MILLIONS

The Circle line is one of the Tube's busiest, with over 114 million journeys a year.

OLD STUFF

The railway infrastructure opened in stages between 1863 and 1884, shown as a separate line on the Tube map from 1949. The line was last extended in 2009 to Hammersmith.

72 MINUTES LONG

As of December 2012, there are six trains per hour, calling at all stations, requiring 18 trains in service at any one time. The journey from Edgware Road around the loop and continuing to Hammersmith takes 72 minutes off-peak.

DEPOT DOGS

The line's depot is at Hammersmith, close to Hammersmith station, originally built by the Great Western Railway to be operated by the Metropolitan Railway when the joint Hammersmith & City Railway was electrified in the early 20th century. Sidings at Barking, Farringdon, and near High Street Kensington (known as Triangle Sidings) stable trains overnight.

MYTHIC TUBES

Owing to its traditionally circular nature, the line has generated many urban myths over the years, including a dead man traveling around undiscovered, a school or office using the service to save infrastructure costs, and, as an April fool in the Independent, a new particle accelerator to coexist alongside passenger services. None of them are true.

DRINKS BAN

A day before a ban on drinking alcohol on public transport in London came into force, a party was held on 31 May 2008, mainly on the Circle line. Thousands of people attended, and 17 were arrested by police due to disorderly behavior, eventually causing several stations to be closed. Perhaps, justifying the ban, really.

10 INTERESTING FACTS ABOUT THE HAMMERSMITH AND CITY

London's second oldest tube line - it opened a year after the Metropolitan Railway - the Hammersmith and City Line has a long and fascinating history. Here are ten interesting facts about the line you may not know.

ONE LINE AND THE SAME

The Hammersmith & City line was shown on the tube map as part of the Metropolitan line until 1990, when it became separated, and the Metropolitan line became the route from Aldgate to Baker Street and northwards through "Metro-land" to Uxbridge, Watford, and Amersham.

THE PINK LINE

This line is printed in pink on the official Tube map and is the color featured around the network.

ROLLING STOCK

Starting in 2015, the signaling system was upgraded as part of a program to increase peak-hour capacity on the line. The six-car C Stock trains were replaced from 2012 to 2014 by new seven-car S Stock trains.

SHARING IS CARING

The line is 15.8 miles (25.5 km) long with 29 stations. Almost all of its track is shared with the other London Underground sub-surface lines: from Hammersmith to Liverpool Street with the Circle line, from Baker Street to Aldgate with the Metropolitan line, and from Aldgate East station to Barking with the District line. All its stations are shared with other lines.

TO BE, OR NOT TO BE

Barbican station replaced a building that claimed that it was originally William Shakespeare's house, although it's never been officially confirmed.

WHAT'S IN A NAME

From 1914 to 2008, Shepherd's Bush Market station was known as Shepherd's Bush. The name was changed to avoid confusing it with the Central and Overground line stations that have the same name.

FAR AWAY

Latimer Road station is half a kilometer (about 1/3 of a mile) away from the road that it is named after.

KIDS THESE DAYS

Barking's modernist ticket hall was built in just 1961, but it has been a protected and listed building since 1995. Whether you appreciate that or not depends on your taste in architecture.

OLD MAN GOWER

Euston Square Station was originally known as Gower Street from 1863 to 1909, when it was renamed Euston Square.

MOST PLATFORMS

Baker Street has the most platforms of any Tube station on the network, with a total of 10 between the various lines that intersect there.

CULTURE

TUBE OF THE IMAGINATION: A GUIDE TO FICTIONAL TUBE STATIONS

It's a common practice in literature and media to create fake places for your stories. Maybe the real ones aren't available or are poorly suited to your movie or show. Perhaps no real place exists that can meet the needs of your story, yet you want everything to be grounded in reality. Being a major world city, London has been subjected to numerous fictional locales in books, radio plays, television, and film. This includes the London Underground, which has seen at least a couple dozen fictional stations. In the case of films and television, many of these were created as the London Underground policy for years made filming in actual stations difficult. With that said, here is a list of many of the fictional Tube stations that have appeared over the years. While not an exhaustive list, this highlights many that you may have seen yourself across television and film.

BLOOMSBURY

This London Underground station was featured in the 1934 crime film Bulldog Jack. A man agrees to pretend to be a famous detective and ends up drawn into a kidnapping scheme. Everything speeds to a conclusion that involves a chase through this fictional station.

COUCH END

You might not have seen this one if you didn't watch the deleted scenes in Shaun of the Dead. The film involves Simon Pegg as Shaun, who must confront the horrors of a zombie apocalypse. Played for laughs, early scenes in the film are devoted to Shaun going about his normal daily routine without realizing that society is breaking down around him. One deleted scene had him waiting for an Underground train at Couch End station. Unlike some on this list, a real Couch End station did once exist but closed in 1954.

HICKORY ROAD

Switching over to literature, the Hickory Road station made its appearance in Agatha Christie's novel Hickory Dickory Dock. Involving detective Hercule Poirot, the story was notably featured in the Poirot television series, which involved a climax chase through the fictional station much like Bulldog Jack.

HOBB'S END

Appearing in the 1967 film version of Quatermass and the Pit, Quartermass discovers an ancient crashed spaceship whose inhabitants prove to be very much alive and not very peaceful. The station is part of the also-fictional Hobb's Lane and tying it when the more horror aspects of the Quatermass series, "Hobb" is actually an ancient name for the devil.

MUSEUM

Not to be confused with British Museum, this station actually featured in the 1972 film Death Line, a horror picture in which

Donald Pleasance plays a detective who discovers a murderous society of cannibals descended from the original Victorian Underground workers.

QUEEN'S ARCADE

As part of the revamped Doctor Who series in 2005, the Ninth Doctor found himself squaring off against the Autons. As the Nestene Consciousness activates a signal that wakes up its warriors all over London, one place where the Autons strike is the fictional Queen's Arcade shopping mall, which includes the also named Underground station.

SUMATRA ROAD

From one popular program to another, the Sumatra Road fictional Tube made an appearance on Sherlock in the episode "The Empty Hearse." The station features as a partially-built but never completed part of the Underground where Holmes and Watson must defuse a bomb that is set to blow up the Houses of Parliament. The station itself is named after the "giant rat of Sumatra" mentioned in the story "The Adventure of the Sussex Vampire."

VAUXHALL CROSS

Certainly not the most popular of the Bond films, 2002's Die Another Day did introduce the fictional station of Vauxhall Cross, which is presumably near the real place where MI6 headquarters is located. While the entrance was across the bridge from the Houses of Parliament in the film, it turns out to be the film's location for Q's gadget lab, in which the eccentric genius presents Bond with his invisible Aston Martin. Interestingly, it is one of many films and shows to film in the disused Aldwych Underground station.

WALFORD EAST

Soap fans will recognize this Tube station as one that connects to possibly their favorite fictional London neighborhood—that of Albert Square in the also fictional Borough of Walford in EastEnders. It replaces the real Bromley-by-Bow Tube station, and most of the platform shops are actually done at East Finchley.

TEN LONDON UNDERGROUND MYSTERIES

The world below the surface has always been a place of mystery, and the same goes for the London Underground. Built in 1863, it was the first underground metropolitan railway in the world. Of course, over time, the Tube has developed its own sub-culture (pun intended), including many urban legends and forgotten lore. From wondering who that mysterious voice is to mass panic caused by fiction, we're having a look at ten bewildering mysteries of the London Underground and what answers exist...if any...

MURDERS ON THE DISTRICT LINE?

At least, that was the subject of John Oxenham's serialized horror novel, A Mystery of the Underground. Published in 1897 in To-day magazine, a series of slayings in the first-class carriage every Tuesday on the District Line prompted real-life Londoners to avoid the Underground 'lest they meet the same fate.

WHO ARE THE GHOSTS OF THE UNDERGROUND?

London is a very haunted city, and this extends to the Tube. Many deaths have been connected to the Underground, whether by their own hand or another's, or building and maintaining the railway, or even from natural causes; it's been said that some of the poor souls never leave. Phantom footsteps have been heard in the Aldgate station late at night. The Bakerloo line passengers sometimes see a ghostly figure sitting next to them in the glass reflection that isn't there when they turn to look. The South Kensington station even once reported a phantom train in 1928. These are but the tip of the iceberg.

A STATION THAT CLOSED BEFORE IT EVER OPENED?

There are many Underground stations that have been closed as ridership declined or new routes made them obsolete. One that never even got a chance is known to staff as Bull & Bush, though its original name was North End. Its name comes from the Bull & Bush Pub nearby, and it was supposed to be part of the Hampstead Heath extension at the turn of the century. However, plans changed after the platforms and lift tunnels had already been constructed, so everything was just bricked up and never used as a station. The station has seen other uses, as it was a storage site for government records during World War 2 and part of London's civil defense preparations during the Cold War.

WHO IS THAT MYSTERIOUS VOICE?

The iconic phrase "Mind the Gap" was introduced in 1968 as a short automated warning chosen due to limited data storage capacity. Sound engineer Peter Lodge had hired an actor to read that line and the command "Stand clear of the closing doors," but the actor wanted royalties, so Lodge recorded his own voice instead. Other stations use different voices, including Emma Clark and Tim Bentinck. Ten stations supplied with announcement systems by PA Communications Ltd. have the voice of Keith Wilson, the firm's industrial sales manager in 1990. The Northern Line used the voice of actor Oswald Laurence until it was gradually phased out. A request from the actor's widow kept his voice at Embankment station so she could still hear it.

WHAT NEW CREATURES EXIST IN THE UNDERGROUND?

Scientists discovered Culex pipiens f. molestus, a new species of mosquito, in the underground in 1998. Living in the tunnels, it mostly prays on rats and mice, and the unfortunate workmen who get bitten occasionally.

WHO IS INSPECTOR SANDS?

Sometimes you may hear an announcement asking for Inspector Sands. The name is actually a coded signal for staff to investigate a fire alarm that has gone off so they can determine the severity rather than create mass panic. The code originated with the theater, but it raises a question of what other codes may exist.

WHAT'S REALLY ON YOUR SEAT?

A forensic investigation of something you use every day can be both fascinating and disgusting. In 2000, scientists in the Department of Forensics at University College London took a row of passenger seats from the Central Line and subjected it to testing. On the surface of the seats, they found the following: four types of hairs (human, mouse, rat, and dog), seven types of insects (mostly still-alive fleas), vomit from nine different people, human urine from four different people, human excrement, rodent excrement, and human semen. Taking the seats apart, they found: the remains of six mice and four rats as well as a brand new type of fungus.

WHERE'S THE SENSE OF HUMOUR?

It's been said that Tube staffers never smile, but they do have their own sense of humor, as sometimes heard by the train announcers. Announcers may occasionally do an American-style announcement to alleviate the boredom. Other times, they may tell off the passenger who doesn't obey the warnings, such as the announcer who proclaimed, "To the gentleman wearing the long gray coat trying to get on the second carriage, what part of 'Stand clear of the closing doors' don't you understand?" If they're feeling particularly cheeky, they may act like an airline pilot instead.

WHAT CAUSED PANIC ATTACKS ON THE CIRCLE LINE?

One urban legend states that the Circle Line, one of the oldest on the Underground, began experiencing major electrical problems in the 1990s. Underground officials and maintenance workers were baffled by the occurrences as they could find nothing wrong. A passenger who'd been riding the Tube for 15 years said that he noticed the disturbances began after leaving the Baker Street station but prior to arriving at Edgeware Road and that the journey between coincided with a rise in general uneasiness and panic attacks. Consulting the British Museum, officials discovered that the area had contained a massive Black Death burial pit. The Underground's solution? A blessing and some holy water, asking workers to refrain from swearing in the area, and replacing the electrical work for the second time in a year. After this, it's said that the disturbances sharply decreased.

WHAT'S BEHIND THE TOWNHOMES ON LEINSTER GARDENS?

23 and 24 Leinster Gardens may look like a pair of ordinary houses from the front, but they're totally fake. In the days of steam-driven Tube trains, the facade was built to hide the smoke as the train emerged from the tunnel to the surface. The BBC program Sherlock made use of this feature in 2014, revealing a fictional hiding space.

6 FASCINATING TUBE STATION NAMES AND THEIR ORIGINS

London is full of interesting names, from streets to boroughs and extending even to the London Underground. The first of its kind in the world, the metro system in London has existed since 1863 and many of its stations have developed some pretty interesting names. Common knowledge of their origins may have been forgotten with time, but often they come from places, people, organizations, or events that happened nearby. If you've found yourself on the Tube and wondered what some of these station names might mean, have a look below for the answers.

ARSENAL

No, the station isn't named for being near any kind of military base or weapons stockpile. The station's original name when it opened was Gillespie Road, so named as that was the street on which the station was located. Things changed in 1913 when Arsenal Football Club moved into the area and established the stadium nearby (now known as Emirates Stadium). Following this, a campaign slowly gained momentum to change the name, which was done in 1932 to Arsenal (Highbury Hill), with the suffix being dropped in 1960.

CANADA WATER

You might think the name is some special connection to the North American nation or perhaps named after a Canadian brand, but the name of one of the Tube's more recent stations is a bit more interesting than that. The name actually comes from the nearby artificial lake, itself located near Canada Dock, a dock that was used mostly by Canadian ships. When the docks closed in the 1970s, the London Dockland Development Corporation took over and built Canada Water lake to help spur the area economically. The area also serves as a wildlife refuge.

COCKFOSTERS

Before you get any cheeky thoughts, the Tube station is one of many named for the nearby area. The area name is a very old one. The area was previously known as "Cock Fosters" and is believed to have originally meant the residence of the cock, or "chief", forester.

MANOR HOUSE

Interestingly, there is no major private estate nearby, but this station actually gets its name from a local public house. The Manor Tavern was built in the area in 1832 and acquired a license for a concert room in 1852, which played host to Queen Victoria at one point in its existence. When the crossroads was widened in 1931, the pub was demolished and rebuilt nearby. The pub closed towards the end of the 20th Century and the building is presently occupied by a grocery store and other businesses.

SEVEN SISTERS

Manor House is actually located on Seven Sisters road, which also lends its name to that Tube station. The name "Seven Sisters" comes from a set of seven trees at the Page Green Common. The story goes that seven sisters who knew that they were bound to part from each other planted seven trees to ensure that they would always be together in same way. For whatever reasons, the trees have occasionally needed to be re-planted, as they have in 1852, 1886, 1955, and 1996.

TOOTING BEC

You're all very rude readers, thinking that this name has something to do with passing wind. The original name for the station was actually Trinity Road (Tooting Bec), and the Tooting Bec part is a very old Saxon name with "Tooting" being "the home of Tota's people". "Bec" is a placename element, though reportedly the name also comes from the land being granted to "Bec Abbey" in France after King William I's conquest of England. Bec was a common placename in Normandy, so it is highly likely that this element for Tooting Bec was influenced by the Abbey.

MANSION HOUSE
PLAISTOW
DAGENHAM EAST
UPMINSTER
GH ST. KENSINGTON

Platform 2

For
take

THE TYPEFACES OF LONDON

Modernity, when it arrives, manifests itself across all culture. When Britain was leaving behind the Victorian era, everything changed, including the lettering used for communication. Influenced by Roman simplicity and Medieval craftsmanship, there was a movement away from the ornate and melodramatic lettering styles of the Victorians towards cleaner, simpler forms that reflected the times. Edward Johnston, and his student and friend Eric Gill, were influenced by the Arts and Crafts Movement, and Johnston revived, almost single-handedly, the art of penmanship and calligraphy. When the London Underground wanted modern lettering to reflect their modern image, they chose Johnston to create it. Inspired by a column from ancient Rome, he designed a typeface that made the signs and posters of the underground system instantly recognizable. With his new sans-serif lettering owned by the Underground, Eric Gill created a similar typeface, which became just as widely used by British Rail, and it was widely distributed as a modern yet classical typeface for a new century.

William Morris and the Arts and Craft Movement was

a 19th-century reaction to the excesses of early industrial production. The Movement promoted traditional craft methods rather than factory production, and it was particularly interested in the Medieval period, when highly-skilled craftsmen worked for themselves, free of factory bosses and production deadlines, to create an object of refinement and beauty. The network of the Movement spread wide and deep, and so there was nothing particularly unusual in the fact that two of Morris' followers, the architect William Harrison Cowlishaw, and William Lethaby, principal of the Central School of Arts and Crafts, both separately met, in 1898, a quiet young man called Edward Johnston.

Johnston was born in Uruguay, but he had been brought up in England by an aunt. His father was a British Cavalry officer, and his mother, Priscilla Buxton, was the daughter of the abolitionist Sir Thomas Fowell Buxton, MP. Home educated, he had followed his own interests and loved mathematics, technology, and practicing the refined handwriting of illuminated manuscripts. When Cowlishaw and Lethaby met him, they encouraged his pursuit of this almost-lost art and advised him to study works at the British Museum. There he discovered the virtues of the broad-edged pen. Difficult to master, this pen has a flat, split nib, unlike the round nib of a modern ball-point. It allows for variations in the thickness of the line created in a continuous, flowing manner – a ribbon of ink.

Lethaby hired Johnston to teach lettering at the Central School, and in 1906 he published a handbook, Writing & Illuminating, & Lettering. Single-handedly he revived the craft of penmanship and developed techniques still used today by amateur and professional practitioners alike.

Public lettering of the time, such as was seen in the advertisements and posters that covered London, was ornate, exaggerated, and designed for impact rather than grace or beauty. So when the commercial manager of the 'Underground Electric Railways Company of London,' Frank Pick, wanted to create a bold image for the new company, which had amalgamated the various independent lines of the London Underground system, the last thing he wanted was lurid Victorian lettering. In 1913

ABCDEFGHIJKLM
NOPQRSTUVWXYZ
abcdefghijklm
nopqrstuvwxyz
1234567890

Gill Sans

he approached Johnston, who had tried but failed to break into the business of creating printing fonts, to create a standard font for the systems signs and notices. His main request was that the lettering should be distinct and not be confused with the advertising posters in the stations and passageways.

Seeking inspiration, Johnston turned to the Column of Trajan in Rome, which celebrated the victory of the Emperor Trajan over the Dacia in the first century AD. The Roman lettering on the column was very highly regarded in the Arts & Crafts Movement. It differed from most other lettering by lacking the short lines at the ends of the strokes, called 'serifs,' that characterize many other forms of lettering. This sans-serif letting was already used in the 19th century, but in a very solid, bold form, with thick strokes, today called grotesques, giving a blocky, attention-seeking form. Johnston's, by contrast, was slender but still substantial – he had found the perfect balance. The type also resembled Caslon, which was created in the 18th century by William Caslon, and is considered the first distinctive English typeface.

ABCDEFGHIJKLM
NOPQRSTUVWXYZ
abcdefghijklm
nopqrstuvwxyz
1234567890

London Tube Typeface

Johnston's font, variously called Underground or Johnston's Railway Type, but today simply called Johnston, was adopted by the Underground, first for printed material, but later for station signs. Johnston also designed the iconic 'bar and circle' logo still in use today by the Underground system.

Johnston's font survived the various re-organizations of the system until 1979 when it became necessary to re-design it due to changes in printing technology. Eiichi Kono, of the design and typography firm of Banks & Miles, created New Johnston, with a wider range of forms, adding Italics, Medium, and Condensed forms to Johnston's simple originals of Regular in upper and lowercase, and Bold, in uppercase only. This is the font currently used in the system. The original Johnston can be seen in archival materials.

Johnston had a student at the Central School called Eric Gill. Gill had been born in Brighton in 1882. He studied church architecture with William Douglas Caroe, another major figure in the Arts & Crafts Movement, who built numerous early 20th century churches in classic styles. Gill found his studies frustrating, and he turned instead to simultaneously studying stonemasonry and calligraphy – the latter with Johnston. He moved to the countryside and established a sculptor's workshop at the village of Ditchling, Sussex. There he created figures based on ecclesiastic church pieces, such as the Madonna. Johnston and his wife joined him at Ditchling, which became a kind of artist's commune.

Gill's career as a typographer began with a commission for an alphabet for the sign-painters of W.H. Smith's, the stationers, and booksellers. A friend, Stanley Morison, was a historian of type who advised the Monotype Corporation, a typeface company that would later develop the ubiquitous modern types of Times New Roman and Arial. Looking for a san-serif type that would rival new German typefaces, he approached Gill to design something for him. He wanted to combine Gill's style based on letters cut into stone with Johnston's Underground Type. Gill's stated aim was to produce a type that was clean, modern, and classical all at the same time. One easily-noticed difference from Johnston's font is the change from diamond-shaped dots on i and j, replacing them with circular dots. Gill worked on the font between 1927 and 1930.

Morison promoted Gill Sans, as the new type was called, and it was quickly adopted first by the London and North Eastern Railway, and then by British Rail. Penguin Books, always promoters of the modern, adopted it for their book covers, and it became – and remains – one of the most popular type faces in England. Monotype created numerous variations and additions over the years. It is considered particularly attractive in uppercase, and for signage, but less so in lowercase, so it is rarely used for text, for example.

Eric Gill went on to a significant career as a sculptor, moving into Art-Deco, when that became popular in the 1930s. Major works can be seen at the BBC's Broadcast House, and above doorways in London and elsewhere. Gill's legacy is less happy, however, as it was revealed in his personal diaries that he sexually abused his daughters, amongst other depravities. There's a movement to have his statues taken down, and for people to stop using his fonts (and use similar ones instead).

Sites to Visit

Ditchling Museum of Art & Craft, Ditchling, East Sussex, contains work by Gill and Johnston, including material related to their fonts.

The London Transport Museum, in the Covent Garden Piazza, WC2, has numerous pieces in Johnston. The Museum is open until 6 pm every day. The London Transport Depot, Acton, has more, but it is only open for special occasions on a few days a year.

If you want to see both typefaces 'in the wild' you only need to go on a stroll around London - you will find both fonts all around you.

As an aside, you may be wondering why we chose to use Gill Sans as the font for this book instead of the official London Underground font. The answer is rather simple, the 'official' Underground font is very, very expensive to license for print. Gill Sans is included with Adobe Fonts.

Further Research

- Writing & Illuminating & Lettering, by Edward Johnston
- Edward Johnston: A Signature for London, by Richard Taylor
- Edward Johnston: Master Calligrapher, by Peter Holliday
- Edward Johnston, by Priscilla Johnston
- Eric Gill, by Fiona MacCarthy
- Eric Gill: Man of Flesh and Spirit, by Malcolm Yorke
- An Essay on Typography, by Eric Gill and Christopher Skelton
- Eric Gill, autobiography, by Eric Gill

THE ABANDONED TUBE

In the 19th Century, the London Underground was created to serve the needs of London's booming suburbs. Today, the Underground (or "Tube" as it's known colloquially) covers 402 kilometres (or 250 miles) of track and 270 stations. Despite having so many Tube stations now, there are many that go unused, having been shut or one reason or another. Here is a list of some really interesting stations along with why they were shut.

BRITISH MUSEUM

While everything in the museum above has been carefully preserved for history, its old Tube station is practically decrepit. Central London Railways opened it in 1900, with the Holborn station opening in 1906, only 100 yards away. Back then, it was common for stations to open up so close in case the railways opted to link service between the stations. However, such plans never materialised and British Museum station fell into disuse and was closed in 1933. It was re-opened for a time during the 1960s as a military administration office and emergency command post, but closed again and stayed shut.

TRAFALGAR SQUARE

On the Bakerloo Line, the Trafalgar Square station opened in 1906. It was used for years until the 1970s when the Jubilee Line was built. With the building of the Charing Cross station, the Trafalgar Square and Strand stations were absorbed into Charing Cross, while some of Trafalgar's lower platforms were wholly abandoned.

CHARING CROSS - JUBILEE LINE PLATFORMS

The station that closed Trafalgar Square station itself closed in 1999. Charing Cross was originally built to be the southern terminus of the Jubilee Line, plans already existed to extend the line to Lewisham in south-east London. After the extension was built, a section of tunnel between Charing Cross and Green Park became a branch line of that new extension. The Charing Cross platforms for the Jubilee line officially shut on 30 November, 1999.

TOWER OF LONDON

Possibly the station with the shortest life of all, it closed in 1884, two years after it opened. It was part of the Metropolitan Railway until 1884 when the District Line and the MR were connected to form the Circle Line. A new station opened at Tower Hill, west of the Tower of London station, which was closed the same day.

UXBRIDGE ROAD

Perhaps one of the oldest on this list, it opened in 1869 as part of the London & North Western Railway and the Great Western Railway. In 1905 it became part of the Metropolitan

Railway and later the Metropolitan Line of the Underground. Ultimately, the station closed after it was bombed in 1940 and never reopened—that is, until a London Overground station, Shepherd's Bush, was built over the old Uxbridge Road site in 2008.

YORK ROAD

Another station opened in 1906, York Road was one of the original stations on the Great Northern, Piccadilly, and Brompton Railway (now simply the Piccadilly Line). It operated infrequently for 26 years until it finally closed in 1932. The reason for the closure is cited as low numbers due to the close proximity to King's Cross St. Pancras and Caledonian Road stations. Amazingly preserved, the building on top of the street sits unused and the station below is still mostly in-tact. There was a plan to potentially re-open it in 2005, but nothing ever came of it.

ALDWYCH

Located on the Piccadilly Line, the line was built as a double track and so Aldwych had two platforms, yet early on, it only ran as a single train shuttle service. Aldwych was closed for six years during World War II where it was used as a bomb shelter. Additionally, it was used as a storage spot for the Elgin Marbles. It was shut in 1994 due to low numbers, but had been threatened with the axe for years and only opened during peak-hours. The last train ran through on 30 September, 1994, 87 years after it first opened. If you've seen a Tube station in TV or movies, it was likely this station as it is often used for filming.

DOWN STREET

Poor, neglected Down Street station. Opened in 1907, it was little used for a couple of decades before it was initially closed in 1932. It was built in the first place for wealthy Mayfair residents, who didn't use it because of a disdainful attitude towards the

Underground. It was practically abandoned and run-down even before it was shut. However, it found some use during World War II as part of the home to Churchill's War Cabinet.

ST. MARY'S

If you go looking for the entrance to St. Mary's Tube station in Whitechapel, you won't find it. It was destroyed by a bomb during the Blitz and the authorities never sought to reopen it. While the entrance is no longer there, underneath the pavement, the interior remains, falling apart and covered in graffiti.

HEATHROW TERMINAL 5

Not exactly shut as such, because it was never really used to begin with. During construction of the Heathrow Terminal 4 Loop in the 1980s, some preparatory work was done in case a fifth terminal was ever built. However, though Terminal 5 was eventually built, the original location planned was about one kilometre away from where the terminal is located currently. The current Terminal 5 station is not where the its predecessor was built.

HOW THE DIFFERENT TUBE LINES GOT THEIR NAMES

Millions of Londoners and tourists use the London Underground every day. They travel from north to south, east to west, and back again along lines with some seemingly unusual names. Bakerloo, Waterloo, Hammersmith & City, the names for the lines on which Tube cars travel, come from history, geography, and special occasions. Most people may not have considered these origins, but once you've finished reading this article, you'll be sure to think about them each time you step into the Underground.

BAKERLOO

The Bakerloo Line goes all the way back to 1865 and the old pneumatic system when it was known as the Waterloo & Whitehall Railway, then the Charing Cross and Waterloo Electric Railway in 1882. Work on the current line began in 1898, and it opened in 1906 as the Baker Street & Waterloo Line, a name that was eventually shortened to simply "Bakerloo."

CENTRAL LINE

The longest of the Underground lines, the Central Line started as the Central London Railway, which opened in 1900 and got its name from the fact that it traveled through Central London on an east-west axis. More interestingly, the Central Line is one that coined the term "Tube" for the Underground. In its earliest days, its shape and the twopenny price for a ride gave it the nickname "Twopenny Tube." As prices increased the "twopenny" part of the nickname was dropped, and "Tube" became the colloquial name that encompassed all of the Underground.

CIRCLE LINE

The Circle Line opened in 1884, and its name comes from the ring that it makes around the city. An extension out to Hammersmith was added in 2009 that creates a more spiraling look.

DISTRICT LINE

The District Line began its life as the District Railway in 1868. It was originally the Metropolitan District Railway, and the idea was that the District Railway would be merged with the Metropolitan Railway, though ultimately, it was decided to keep them separate as it would be easier to raise funds for the District Railway separately. It is from this original "Metropolitan District" combined name that the District Line gets its name, as the Metropolitan Railway came first and kept its original name.

ELIZABETH LINE

Originally dubbed Crossrail, and not technically a 'tube' line, the Elizabeth Line was named after the late Queen Elizabeth II. Opening the line in person was amongst the last of her public duties in summer 2022.

HAMMERSMITH & CITY LINE

The Hammersmith & City Line earns part of its name from its most western stop in Hammersmith. The name originated as applied to the Hammersmith & City Railway that opened in 1864 and only applied to a three-mile section of track between the Hammersmith and Westbourne Park stations that was operated jointly by the Metropolitan and Great Western Railways until 1868. From then on, it was not shown as a separate line on the Tube map until 1990.

JUBILEE LINE

Jubilee is the youngest line in the Underground, and its name has a very special significance. Like Most of the other lines, it was originally part of the Metropolitan Railway. In 1971, construction began on the new "Fleet" Line to help ease some of the congestion for travelers coming from suburbs in Northwest London. With the Silver Jubilee of Queen Elizabeth II coming up in 1977, the suggestion was made in 1975 to rename the line "Jubilee" in her honor. At first, the recommendation was shot down as being too costly, but a victory by the Conservatives in the Great London Council Election of 1977 resulted in the change happening anyway, as the candidates had made the change part of their campaign platforms. The line is also colored silver in reference to this event.

METROPOLITAN LINE

The Metropolitan Line is the oldest of the Underground lines, having opened in 1863 as the first underground railway in the world. The name is in recognition of London's status as the largest city in the world for much of the 19th Century. The line is also known as the "Met" and even inspired the French Metropolitan, which imitated the name from London.

NORTHERN LINE

The Northern Line came about as a result of the integration of the City & South London Railway and the Charing Cross, Euston, & Hampstead Railway beginning in the 1920s, though both railways existed as early as 1890. It was officially named the "Northern" Line in 1937 in recognition of a planned addition of a "Northern Heights" railway extension. The plans for the extension were eventually abandoned in 1954, but the line kept the name.

PICCADILLY LINE

Like many of the early Underground lines, the Piccadilly line had quite a long name when it opened in 1906 as the Great Northern, Piccadilly, & Brompton Railway. The line was formed out of a merger between the Great Northern & Strand Railway and the Brompton & Piccadilly Circus Railway, and over time, the other parts of the name dropped away until the entire line came to reference the Piccadilly Circus station, which itself is named after the Piccadilly House which one existed on the road junction above the station.

VICTORIA LINE

Before the Jubilee Line opened in 1979, the Victoria Line was the youngest in the Underground, having opened only 11 years prior in 1968. A Working Party set up by the British Transportation Commission recommended the line as an extension to help relieve congestion by establishing a line to run from Walthamstow Station to Victoria Station, the latter of which is where the line gets its name. The station's name comes from Victoria Street above the station, which, as you may guess, is named for Queen Victoria.

WATERLOO & CITY LINE

The original line followed the London & South Western Railway, which within London had a station near Waterloo Bridge. The Waterloo Bridge Station eventually became shortened to Waterloo, but both reference the Battle of Waterloo, in which the Duke of Wellington was the leader of the British forces that worked in an alliance with other European nations to deliver a final defeat to Napoleon.

WAY
OUT

TOP 10 THINGS TO LOVE ABOUT THE TUBE

The Tube is another one of those iconic London landmarks that I love to bits. I got to thinking – just what is it about the Tube that I love so much? Here are ten things I love about the Tube in no particular order.

IT GOES EVERYWHERE

The Tube simply goes everywhere – with 250 miles of track and 270+ stations, the London Underground sprawls in every direction. You can travel to a different station every day and discover something new.

MIND THE GAP

The most iconic phrase to come from the Tube is 'Mind the Gap,' which is broadcast over audio systems of the network and also painted on the platforms. It's such a reassuring thing to hear the tone and then the calm voice warning you to watch your step as you get on the train.

THE SMELL

Some would argue that the Tube doesn't smell good. But I would argue that the Tube has its own unique patina – dust, engines, and people all combine to make the smell of the London Underground completely unique. I know I'm in London when the smell hits me at Heathrow station.

THE WHOOSH

One of the simple pleasures of traveling in London is standing on the platform, hearing the train approach, and then feeling the rush of wind rushing ahead of the train as it arrives. It's such a feeling of anticipation. And a relief on a hot day as most of the Underground is not air-conditioned!

OLD STATIONS

While there are no shortages of new stations on the network, I really love visiting the old stations – some built over a hundred years ago. Many have unique and beautiful tile work you simply cannot see anywhere else. There's such a timelessness about these stations, and they're a joy to travel through.

THE TUBE MAP

With 270+ stations, it would be easy to get confused when you look at a rail map. That's why Harry Beck had the brilliant idea to re-imagine the map as an electrical diagram, and the iconic Tube Map was born. It's so simple to navigate – you can easily find your way around London and transferring between lines.

IT'S A CHEAP WAY TO GET AROUND LONDON

There are cheaper ways to get around London (buses are much cheaper), but the Tube is a surprisingly affordable way to travel around London when you're on a budget. When we visited during our college days, it was indispensable for poor college students.

FEEL LIKE A LOCAL

We know it will never be possible for us to live in London, but when we travel there – riding the Underground makes us feel like locals. You get to see a slice of London life. London fashion. What people are reading. Hear what people are listening too. You also notice social cues you might not notice anywhere else (like don't talk, ever, or don't sit next to someone if there is a free seat elsewhere).

THE OYSTER CARD

London pioneered using an electronic card to travel its network, and we recommend that everyone get one before they go to London. It never expires, and you can use it on future trips. For those that don't know what it is – the Oyster card is your ticket to the Tube. It gives you the cheapest fare whenever you use it (and caps out for multiple trips). It's much cheaper to use than paper tickets. It's also much easier to use to get through the ticket barriers. My Oyster card is one of my prized possessions, and I always keep it with my passport, ready to go to London.

THE ROLLING STOCK

I'm not a train geek that can tell you what kind of train each one is, but I simply love trains and love examining the variety across the network. They're so fast! And that sound they make as they accelerate out of the station is truly an iconic London sound.

DOWN STREET TUBE ABANDONED STATION - CHURCHILL'S SECRET WARTIME BUNKER

London's abandoned Tube stations have a special aura about them. It's hard to believe that in a city of eight million people, some tube stations were not used enough to justify staying open. But just because a stationed is abandoned, doesn't mean it can't serve a purpose. And when war is a certainty, every available underground space all of a sudden becomes important. Churchill's Cabinet War Rooms are very much well-known, and you can visit them to this day, but what many don't know is that until they were ready for his use, he had another secret bunker – Down Street Tube Station. We had the chance to explore this dark and dangerous place on an organized tour last February. It was a once-in-a-lifetime opportunity.

As with every Tube station, it was originally built with great optimism. The first lines of the London Underground were privately built and funded, so each station was meant to be a money-making proposition. With great fanfare, Down Street Tube Station opened up in 1907 by the Great Northern, Piccadilly and Brompton Railway. It was latterly served by the Piccadilly line and was situated between Dover Street (now

24
MAYFAIR MINI MAR
DOWN STREET
MEWS W1
Coca-Cola
Leander
Leander
SANDWICHES
SOFT DRINKS

named Green Park) and Hyde Park Corner stations. It was designed by Leslie Green in the beautiful Arts & Crafts style of other Piccadilly Line stations. It was thought that a station located just off Pall Mall would be popular with the wealthy residents and guests at the world-class hotels located nearby.

What they didn't figure was that wealthy people had no desire to ride the Tube. They had their own means to get around London. The station entrance was also poorly placed because the only place they could fit a station entrance was on Down St, a few hundred feet from Pall Mall itself. Dover St and Hyde Park Corner Stations were not too far away anyway, so people just used those instead. It was simply too inconveniently located to be useful to anyone. As a consequence, the station was little used and was closed in 1932.

Then the war came.

It started to look like war was a distinct possibility in 1938 and preparations began to shore up Britain's infrastructure to ensure continued operations during any kind of attack. Britain's Railways were its most important national asset so it was decided that the Railway Executive Committee (REC) would be formed to get the railways on a war footing. At this stage in Britain's rail history, this was pre-nationalization, so all the different rail lines were privately owned and privately competing; they weren't exactly keen to work together. So, it was up to the REC to coordinate amongst the various organizations to ensure continued operations.

The REC needed a secured telephone exchange to allow it to communicate quickly with the various railway companies. It needed bomb proofing and they need space for the Committee to meet and work 24 hours a day. The plan was to put this new exchange in the basement of their original Westminster headquarters, but this was deemed unsafe due to flooding risk and the fact the building could not withstand a 500lb bomb blast. They thought about putting it somewhere in London's suburbs, but they really needed to be as close to the government as possible. Someone had the bright idea that there was a perfectly good Tube station, unused and close to London's poshest hotels and restaurants.

It did not take much to convince the patrician REC Committee Member that this was the ideal solution. A large sum of money was spent to convert the entire below-ground station into their new wartime headquarters. The telephone exchange was installed. The elevator shaft and tunnels were reinforced, and living accommodations were installed. The place was to be manned 24 hours, seven days a week. Due to its sensitive nature, employees were required to live on-site during their shifts so that the comings and goings wouldn't be obvious to would-be spies. It didn't even have its own postal address. Dispatches had to be sent via a crack team of motorcyclists always on call, some of whom were women.

The place served its purpose well, and Britain's railways were able to continue operating during the war, some would say better than before the war! The entire place was a self-contained community with all the provisions they would need (outside of the ration system, I should add). There was a staff canteen which was known to have good food, and there was kitchen staff on duty at all hours.

During the London Blitz, which lasted from September 1940 to March 1941, no part of London was safe from German bombs. That included Downing St, the official residence of the Prime Minister, which was heavily damaged during the bombing raids. His bunker at the Cabinet War Rooms was not ready. The most important man in Britain needed somewhere to sleep. The brother of the REC Chair, Sir Ralph Wedgwood convinced Churchill that he would be the safest in the REC's emergency headquarters at Down St.

Churchill spent a total of forty nights during the Blitz in Down Street, taking over the office of one of the committee members as sleeping quarters. The railway hotels serviced the facility, so the food and drink were up to Churchill's standard, and it was said that he rather liked the accommodations; he always made the best of any situation as best he could. He liked the place so much that he arranged to have new personal quarters built for his future use. Alas, they went unused as once the Cabinet War Rooms were completed, he did not need to visit Down St again.

ENQUIRIES & COMMITTEE ROOM

TO THE TRA

After the war, the REC no longer needed the facility, and it was returned to the London Underground, which used it as an engineering access area for the Piccadilly Line. Most of the fittings and fixtures from the war were removed, but elements remain in place, an eerie reminder of Britain's wartime past. The most amazing treasure down there are the remains of the telephone exchange, a beautiful piece of mechanical 20th-century engineering history. There are other bits and bobs from its human habitations, from bathtubs, boilers, and the ruins of the kitchen. It's very bizarre to think of all the people working down here, doing their bit for the war as bombs well down from above.

We went down in a tour group of ten people, from all over Britain – and even one fellow who flew in from the Netherlands – so it was an intimate tour. Our tour guide has done the tour almost 100 times, so he's old hat. The station is not suitable for 'tourist' consumption. It's dark, dirty, and dangerous. If a Tube train passed, we had to turn out our flashlights, which made it even darker. It was dusty, loud, and beautiful. The station is occasionally open for tours through Hidden London, part of the London Transport Museum. The tickets often sell out a year or so in advance, but you can keep an eye on their website to find out when tickets will be available again. If you have any interest in London's transport and wartime history, I cannot recommend doing this tour more highly.

THE LONDON TUBE ON FILM

When a movie is set in London, inevitably, the Tube will make an appearance. Here's a list of films where the Tube plays an outsized role in the plot (it is not an exhaustive list of every screen appearance of the Tube).

London's underground railway system, known as the Tube, has featured in several films. The plot of the 1998 film Sliding Doors hinges on whether Gwyneth Paltrow's character catches a particular Tube train or not. Bulldog Jack (1934), Man Hunt (1941), The Good Die Young (1954), and 28 Weeks Later (2007) all include chase sequences across underground tracks.

A number of horror films have also used the subterranean network of tunnels as an atmospheric location, most notably the John Landis hit An American Werewolf in London (1981) (#1 in U.S.), which contains a famous scene set in Tottenham Court Road tube station, and the 2004 film Creep. The eerie 1973 horror Death Line stars Donald Pleasence as a Scotland Yard detective who traces a series of murders to cannibals living in the network's tunnels.

Excavations on the Underground unearthed an ancient alien spacecraft in Quatermass and the Pit (1967), and dormant dragons in Reign of Fire (2002).

The 2002 James Bond film Die Another Day features a secret MI6 facility in a fictional disused Underground Station called Vauxhall Cross. The 2012 Bond film Skyfall sets a long chase scene in the London Underground near a makeshift underground MI6 base near the Old Bailey. Another fictional station, Hobbs End, features in the 1967 science fiction film Quatermass and the Pit. Deleted scenes for Shaun of the Dead features the fictional Crouch End station.

Other films to have featured the Underground include Passport to Pimlico (1949), The Yellow Balloon (1953), Georgy Girl (1966), The Fourth Protocol (1987), Hidden City (1988) and Tube Tales (1999). The makers of the children's film The Boy Who Turned Yellow (1972) managed to persuade London Underground to paint a tube train yellow.

Maida Vale Tube stations plays a nice role in the love story of the couple in About Time (2013), as they story is told through montages at the station.

A rare recreation of the network in the Edwardian era featured in the adaptation of Henry James's The Wings of the Dove in 1997. The London underground of the 1920s is also recorded in Anthony Asquith's silent classic Underground (1928), while the 1969 film Battle of Britain shows the tunnel network converted to provide shelter for Londoners during the Blitz.

Aldwych tube station, formerly on a branch of the Piccadilly line, has been used as the location for many films and television productions, especially since the branch and station closed in 1994 and the platforms have been left intact making it suitable for filming and photography purposes, due to the absence of a regular train service. A 1970s tube train is permanently based at the station, and heritage rolling stock can be brought in for filming - London Underground have retained one of their 1938 trains which can be used for historic appearances. In more recent years, filming has also taken place at the former Jubilee line platforms at Charing Cross station,[2] which were withdrawn from regular use when the line was extended in 1999 avoiding the station.

Here's a list of films where the Tube has made an appearance:

- Underground (1928)
- Bulldog Jack (1935)
- Passport to Pimlico (1949)
- Train of Events (1949)
- Seven Days to Noon (1950)
- Georgy Girl (1966)
- Press for Time (1966)
- Daleks - Invasion Earth 2150 AD (1966)
- Quatermass and the Pit (1967) — fictional station Hobbs End
- Battle of Britain (1969)
- The Bed-Sitting Room (1969)
- Death Line (aka Raw Meat) (1972)
- Hanover Street (1979)
- An American Werewolf in London (1981)
- Lifeforce (1985)
- The Fourth Protocol (1987)
- Superman IV: The Quest for Peace (1987)
- Hidden City (1988)
- The Krays (1990)
- Patriot Games (1994)[3]
- Mission: Impossible (1996)
- Secrets & Lies (1996)
- The Wings of the Dove (1997)
- Croupier (1998)
- Sliding Doors (1998)

- Tube Tales (1999)
- Virtual Sexuality (1999)
- The End of the Affair (1999)
- Billy Elliot (2000)
- Bridget Jones's Diary (2001)
- Die Another Day (2002) — fictional station Vauxhall Cross
- Reign of Fire (2002)
- 28 Days Later (2002)
- Mujhse Dosti Karoge! (2002)
- Bend It Like Beckham (2002)
- Love Actually (2003)
- Code 46 (2003)
- The Mother (2003)
- Shaun of the Dead (2004) — fictional station Crouch End
- If Only (2004)
- Touch of Pink (2004)
- Creep (2004)
- Agent Cody Banks 2: Destination London (2004)
- The Football Factory (2004)
- Green Street (2005)
- V for Vendetta (2005)
- The Good Shepherd (2006)
- 28 Weeks Later (2007)
- Harry Potter and the Order of the Phoenix (2007)
- Atonement (2007)
- The Bourne Ultimatum (2007)
- Three and Out (2008)
- The Edge of Love (2008)
- The Escapist (2008)
- Skyfall (2012) — Temple and fictional train derailment
- Darkest Hour (2017)

THE LONDON TUBE ON TV

While the Tube has made prolific appearances in film, it's also played a starring role on television, appearing in many American and British TV shows alive.

Here's a list of shows where the Tube plays a key role:

Doctor Who

- The Dalek Invasion of Earth (1964)
- The Web of Fear (1967)
- Invasion of the Dinosaurs (1974)
- The Trial of a Time Lord (Parts 1-4) (1986)
- "Rose" (2005) — fictional station

Others

- Game On
- The setting for 'The Lab' HQ of The Tomorrow People (1973–1979)

- The setting of EastEnders features the fictitious Walford East tube station replacing Bromley-by-Bow.
- CGI "Underground Ernie"
- Primeval (2007)
- Thunderbirds featured Tube stations, but they were deserted due to the series being set in the future.
- Spooks (series 7) (2008)
- The F Word (2008)
- Mr. Selfridge (2013)
- Sherlock (2014)

In addition to its role in fiction, there have also been several TV documentaries about the Tube that are available to watch, you can find most of these on the various streaming services or on YouTube. Here's a quick list:

- The Tube (2012): A BBC documentary about the London Underground
- The Tube (2003): The Tube is a British television program shown on ITV London. It is a documentary/docusoap about the London Underground network and follows London Underground workers—drivers, station staff, managers, and so forth—showing the Underground system to the public through their eyes.
- Secrets of the London Underground (2021-2022): Secrets of the London Underground is a British factual documentary series presented by railway historian Tim Dunn and London Transport Museum's Engagement Manager, Siddy Holloway.
- How they Dug the Victoria Line (1969)
- The Tube: Going Underground (2016)
- Inside the Tube: Going Underground (2017)
- Keeping London Moving: Then and Now
- The Tube: An Underground History (2013)
- The Fifteen Billion Pound Railway
- Ghosts on the Underground
- Metroland

- Secrets of Underground London (PBS)

PICCADILLY RLY
STRAND STATION
Fire exit Keep clear
Fire exit Keep clear

EXPLORING ALDWYCH ABANDONED TUBE STATION

It's hard to imagine that in this modern day and age that there would be anywhere in London that's abandoned, forgotten, and out of use. Until very recently, London was home to the most expensive real estate on the planet. But yet, there are pockets of London that are abandoned. The London Underground is home to several abandoned Tube Stations. These so-called 'ghost stations' went out of service for many different reasons, but there are several of them, and occasionally they're opened up for tours for curious Londonphiles to explore.

Hidden London is a program run by the London Transport Museum that provides the opportunity for enthusiasts to explore the old or abandoned parts of the Tube network that are no longer in use. One would think that something like this would be a bit of a niche interest, but whenever they offer tickets for these tours, they sell out within minutes. It's something I've personally always wanted to do. There's a certain romance about abandoned Tube stations, forgotten to history, covered in the dust of Londoners past and present. It's no surprise that many of these are used as ad hoc shooting locations for TV shows and films.

Hidden London is a program run by the London Transport Museum that provides the opportunity for enthusiasts to explore the old or abandoned parts of the Tube network that are no longer in use. One would think that something like this would be a bit of a niche interest, but whenever they offer tickets for these tours, they sell out within minutes. It's something I've personally always wanted to do. There's a certain romance about abandoned Tube stations, forgotten to history, covered in the dust of Londoners past and present. It's no surprise that many of these are used as ad hoc shooting locations for TV shows and films.

When a new round of Hidden London tours was announced last fall, I prepared for disappointment; I always managed to miss out on getting tickets. I keep an eye on these things since I am a Tube enthusiast. I knew what time they were being released, and I knew to be at the computer ready to buy. My goal was to tour Down Street station, famous for being a bunker during World War II for Churchill's wartime government. Sadly, it was sold out before my fingers could move fast enough. I tried the second station on offer and was similarly locked out. I clicked into the third option for tours of Aldwych Station and with luck, it was not sold out – in fact, there were plenty of options available in February 2016 (about five months from when I was booking). I immediately booked a ticket for the tour and couldn't believe my luck.

Then it hit me; I just bought tickets to a tour that would require me to book an entire trip to Britain from the USA. I take my interest in the Tube very seriously. The months passed, and I booked a trip to London using my hard-earned airline miles. And on Saturday, February 20, I found myself standing in a queue outside Aldwych Abandoned Tube station waiting to get inside. It was all very surreal and exciting.

The first question probably running through your head is why would they ever close a Tube station? The story of Aldwych is not typical of the Underground. When the various Tube lines were built, they were built by competing companies (with a profit motive). Aldwych was opened in 1907 with the name Strand,

WAY OUT
CLOSED
UNDERGROUND
STATION
CLOSED
UNDERGROUND

after the street on which it is located, and was the terminus of the short Piccadilly line branch from Holborn that was a relic of the merger of two railway schemes. Over the years, there were many plans to make the station a through station to connect it to the rest of the network, but it remained a dead end of sorts for the Piccadilly line and due to low passenger volume, it was eventually closed in 1994 (the elevators needed to be replaced and the cost of doing so exceeded the profits generated by passengers using the station). The guides joked that the station was now making more money than it ever did doing semi-regular tours.

Our tour began in the entry hallways, where the staff explained the history of the station and why it was closed. The guides were a fountain of knowledge on the various decorations and architectural styles. The style of the station very much matches the styles of other Piccadilly line stations. The entryway features lovely green tiles, and over the years, the station has also been a testing ground for designs used in future stations.

There were about 20 fellow Tube enthusiasts on the tour – all with high-powered cameras clicking and clacking away. It was such a rare treat to be able to explore the station that there was an air of excitement. It was one of many tours that day, yet the staff never appeared bored or annoyed at all the tourists wanting to poke around their station.

After introductory remarks, it was time to descend to the out-of-service platforms. Since the Victorian elevators no longer worked, visitors were required to descend 160 or so steps to the platforms. This wasn't so bad going down, and it went by quite quickly. Going back up when the tour was over was quite exhausting, and I felt quite sorry for the heavily pregnant woman in front of me who had to climb back up!

The most interesting aspect of the station's history was its use as a bomb shelter during both World War I and World War II. Many people don't realize that the Blitz in World War II was not the first time that Londoners had to shelter from German bombs. World War I also featured several great Zeppelin raids that inflicted mass damage on London. Aldwych proved useful as a shelter not once, but twice (and let's hope never again).

During World War II, one of the disused platforms was used to store art from the National Gallery. It's rather an interesting thought to think of the nation's Turners and Constables chilling out on a disused Tube platform. It turns out, though, that the damp station wasn't the best place to store valuable paintings, so they shifted to the storage of statues and other works of art that wouldn't be damaged by water (looking up you can see the calcite deposits leaking from the ceiling – art doesn't like that!)

The most famous tenants during World War II were the Elgin Marbles from the British Museum. The Marbles were originally from the Parthenon in Greece and Britain's possession of them is controversial. Despite this, Britain has cared for them well and stored them for protection when needed. The guides told us how they had to be winched down with a crane through the elevator shaft. When they were removed after the war, they decided this was too dangerous to repeat so they took them out by train to a neighbouring station where they could be more easily removed. The other platforms were used to house people sheltering from bombs during the London Blitz (which took place at the end of 1940) and the V1 and V2 raids later in the war.

I was most interested in the station's use as a shelter during World War II. The station was not particularly deep, so the residents of the shelter would still have had the terrifying experience of hearing bombs dropping all around them as it was in the center of London. Conditions for those in the shelter were not great – people would have to queue for hours for a place and sometimes they did not get them. Racks of beds were provided for people to sleep, the platforms were closed, so hammocks were strung across the tracks. Facilities were very basic at first – a bucket sufficed as a toilet at the beginning (though this changed later on).

The British with their Blitz spirit would make the most of the situation; children would play together. Sometimes concerts were held from the station and broadcast to the rest of the country as a propaganda move to show that Britain was not afraid. Simply acting like nothing was amiss was crucial to maintain good morale as Britain faced its most existential threat.

UNDERGROUND

At one point during the war, more than 100,000 people were sheltering in Tube stations all over the network. At first, the British government did not want people to do this – but as there were no adequate deep level bomb shelters, they relented and began to allow the stations to be used as long as it didn't interfere with London's wartime transport needs.

While the facilities were basic at the beginning, by 1941, there was a first aid post, proper latrines (instead of the bucket), a canteen that wasn't subject to rationing, (which meant all the hot yummy food you could eat) a library, and other entertainments. It was all about making a home away from home to make the situation bearable.

Londoners made the best of their time in the shelter – there was plenty to do when you weren't sleeping, though that's what most people did (in between copious amounts of tea). As the war progressed and the Blitz officially ended, use of the station as a shelter tapered off. It went up again during the V1 and V2 raids in the latter part of the war. The public shelter closed when the war ended in May 1945.

As the station is in a disused condition, it is very much as it was in the 1940s as the station has not had updates familiar to later Tube stations. This gives you a unique look at how life would have been like during its use as a bomb shelter during the wars. The tour was good enough to highlight this and even had recordings of people who remembered their experiences sheltering in the Tube.

After the war, passenger service was not restored until 1946. And even then, passenger numbers were very low – it was never a widely used station because not many people lived in the neighborhood it served. There were no major tourist attractions nearby and many workers used other Tube stations (some of which were quicker to walk to than to take a train to). So after the war, the station became a testing bed for future Tube station designs (examples of which you can see on the tour).

Since the station was essentially a dead end on the Piccadilly line, it was not widely used when it was re-opened. It was kept open for convenience sake, but by the early 1990s, it was clear that keeping the station open was a waste of public money. So, the station was locked up and the passengers were told to go to neighboring stations. Since the station was closed, it has had a second life as a shooting location for film and TV.

If you're a fan of British TV and film, this station will look very familiar to you. Whenever a TV show or film crew needs a Tube station, they'll usually hire Aldwych. There's even a full-scale Tube train gathering dust at one of the platforms suitable for filming use. What films have used the station? "Atonement," "V for Vendetta," "28 Weeks Later", and "The Imitation Game" amongst others were filmed in the station. There are artifacts from the filming all around the station (there are many posters and advertisements that don't belong there but were left by careless film crews). The hit TV shows "Sherlock" and "Mr Selfridge" have also made use of the station many times. The station is also used as a training facility for the Tube's emergency services.

You get a rather eerie feeling walking through the silent and dimly lit corridors of the disused station. You can feel the ghosts of London's past as you explore the empty station. There's a very lovely smell – a combination of grime and dust that could only be in a place that was touched by many layers of peoples lives through history. It's a terrifying prospect to imagine being sheltered there during World War II and it makes one grateful that such a thing is not necessary anymore.

Overall, I was very pleased with the Hidden London tour. The staff were friendly, knowledgeable, and a bit funny as well. The London Transport Museum will continue to run Hidden London tours throughout the year. It's best to sign up on its website to find out when the tours will be. I definitely want to try and explore some of the other disused stations, such as the one at Down Street where Churchill's government holed up during German air raids. There's also a deep level shelter in Clapham open occasionally that was used during the war and also for refugees after the war. The guides assured us that Aldwych would be on future tours so you can have the same opportunity to explore London's history as I did.

THE SIX OLDEST UNDERGROUND STATIONS STILL IN USE

It's difficult to imagine a time when you couldn't move about London on the Tube. Lobbied for by City of London Solicitor Charles Pearson and designed by John Fowler, it was a marvel of its time and became the basis for other great cities' underground railway systems. Six stations opened on 10 January 1863 as part of the original Metropolitan Line that are still in operation today. Here's an overview of these six stations.

1. BAKER STREET

A location known primarily for a famous fictional detective's residence, it started with just two platforms, but was expanded decades later to include two more lines. Its services have been expanded several times to where it not only includes the Metropolitan line but also serves Hammersmith and City, Circle, Bakerloo, and Jubilee. As a nod to the area's famous fictional resident, the station is decorated with profile silhouettes of Sherlock Homes. Outside the Marylebone exists there is a also a statue of the detective.

2. EUSTON SQUARE

The station opened as "Gower Street" on 10 January , but eventually changed the name to Euston Square in 1909. It should not be confused with the nearby Euston tube station for the Northern and Victoria lines.

3. FARRINGDON

The original terminus of the Metropolitan Railway, Farringdon was originally known as "Farringdon Street." It was relocated in 1865 as the MR opened an extension to Moorgate and was renamed "Farringdon & High Holborn" in 1922, a name it kept until 1936. The railway entrance has been rebuilt a couple of times and the most recent upgrade came as part of the plan to accommodate Thameslink trains which should be complete in 2018. The Moorgate branch was severed in 2009 and the station currently serves the Metropolitan, Circle, and Hammersmith & City lines.

4. GREAT PORTLAND STREET

It opened as "Portland Road" in 1910 and experienced two name changes over time, first to "Great Portland Street and Regents Park" in 1923 and then to its current name in 1917. The entrance of the station was built in 1930 on Marylebone Road and owes its round shape to being built on a traffic island. The above ground part of the station has shops on the first floor and offices on the second, and even once included a car dealership with a showroom as Great Portland Street was big location for the motor industry. Today it serves not only the Metropolitan line, but Circle and Hammersmith & City lines as well.

5. KING'S CROSS ST. PANCRAS

Current Piccadilly Platforms, Original Platforms Now Disused.

Serving King's Cross station opened with the others on 10 January 1863 and has been rearranged a couple of times in 1868 and 1922. It has perhaps the most gruesome history of the original stations as a fire in 1987 believed to have been caused by a matching dropping into an escalator machine room killed 31 people. It was also one of the locations attacked on the 7 July 2005, in which a bomb killed 26 people as the train traveled between the station and Russell Square. Its location means it is a heavily used line and not only serves Metropolitan, Circle, and Hammersmith & City lines, but the Northern, Victoria, and Piccadilly lines as well.

6. PADDINGTON

Another on the list that has a tie not only to the underground but also the Great Western Railway, it was originally the terminus for the Metropolitan line coming from Farringdon. While no longer part of the Metropolitan line, it instead serves the Bakerloo, Circle, District, and Hammersmith & City lines. Like Baker Street, Paddington also has ties to a famous fictional character as Michael Bond named his creation Paddington Bear after the underground station he regularly used to get home from his job as a BBC cameraman. A statue of the famous bear made by Marcus Cornish can be found under the clock on platform 1 of the railway station.

bauhaus

A LOVE LETTER TO THE TUBE

The Tube Station at Heathrow Terminal Five is relatively new when you consider the overall age of the London Underground. This is often your first introduction to the Tube, and that's fine. Better a brand new station than an old one. When presented with the options of getting from well-connected Heathrow into central London, you realize you perhaps didn't bring enough money with you on your trip. A taxi is almost a hundred dollars. The Heathrow Express, the other train to Paddington, is £25 one way. It's the most expensive rail journey in Britain by track length versus cost. A bus does not appeal. So, you opt for the Tube - the cheapest option.

It's a deceiving ride at the start because the train is practically empty. You get comfortable, thinking that you'll have it to yourself. Buckle in and get ready, because this is the longest way into central London and will take at least forty-five minutes. As you leave the tunnels of Heathrow, the train fills with the warmth of that English sun for which you came all this way. It's slightly disorienting - you thought the Tube was all underground? Well, it's not. Out in the suburbs, or the outer zones, the Tube is mostly above ground. It only goes underground when it gets more toward central London.

From this vantage point - you get a strange view of London you weren't expecting and the guidebooks don't tell you about. You're seeing what London is really like for the people who live there. It's the back garden tour of London. Some back gardens are nicer than others. You see the uniformity in London's architecture that varies from Victorian to Edwardian, to post-war Modernist, to modern glass box tower blocks. You can't help but think large parts of this area of London look slightly shabby. You're not wrong in thinking this. London is not a gleaming, perfect city - even in its tourist heart.

You're tired after your transatlantic flight. It's early. The sun is nice, but you can't help nodding off a bit as the train rocks back and forth as it speeds towards central London. But you never fall asleep, because the train is always coming to a gentle stop, thanks to the skill of your Tube driver to pick up more passengers. It's not safe to fall asleep anyway. You hold your bag closer and closer as more people get on. You begin to think about the end of your journey; it's still pretty early, and you know your hotel won't be ready until the afternoon. All you want to do is sleep, but you can't.

You're in London, how could you sleep?

No one talks to you. Everyone minds their own business on the Tube. People read books, listen to music (some a bit too loud, you tut), read the free *Metro* newspaper, or just zone off into space, knowing they'll be at work soon. You're not at work.

You're in London for fun, which the locals may find a bit odd.

This is all a novelty for you, but it's not for them. They don't really even care that you're there, except they're slightly annoyed when they see your luggage taking up so much space on the train. Your bag is probably too big, but packing for London is always a challenge. No matter how hard you try, you can't fit everything into a single carry-on bag. You did your best. Best to just ignore the glares. They will get worse the closer you get to central London.

"Please mind the gap," the announcer occasionally says as

the train stops at stations with the most London-y names you can imagine.

Uxbridge.

Sudbury Hill.

Park Royal.

North Ealing.

Hammersmith.

The places sound like magical, fantasy names in a Tolkien book. You wonder what exciting things there are in these places. In all honesty, there isn't much of interest there for you, the tourist. These are places Londoners live. They're delightfully banal. Streets are filled with rows of houses that look similar. High streets are filled with charity shops, fried chicken shops, fish and chip shops, and other fast food chains. And the bookmakers, taking bets on everything. A lot of the time, they're not very nice places. You can understand why you keep hearing about the "death of the high street," because even the people who live there don't really want to visit them. Not everyone can live in a twee village with a posh high street.

"Please mind the gap." It's a soothing phrase. You don't remember hearing anyone tell you to be careful on your public transport system back home.

Then, the light of London's sun is gone.

You go underground somewhere near or around Earl's Court.

You really begin to wonder about these place names. Who is Earl? And what's in his court? Do they mean Earl in the titled Earl of Grantham sense or Earl as in the bloke's name was Earl? Was there a palace where Earl held court? Or is it a tennis court? You've heard it's a cheap neighborhood near central London,. but you've also been warned away from there by several people. So, you picked somewhere else to stay. This is where you go back underground.

The train seems to go faster when it goes through the dark tunnels. The warm London sunlight is banished by the darkness of the tunnels, and now you have artificial lighting to bear down on you. Now, there's only room to stand. You cannot get your bag any closer to you. You hope the Londoners don't hate you right now. Most probably aren't even paying attention to you at all - just another tourist in the way. It's a shame transatlantic flight arrivals coincide with rush hour on the Tube. Even though the train is packed, you could almost hear a pin drop, save for the noise of the train and the tunnels outside.

People start to get off the train, but it seems even more people get back on.

Your stop is close; you can feel it. You've been watching the map above the door for almost the whole journey. It gave you something to look it, so you didn't look with too much curiosity at the Londoners around you. You start to hear names you've heard in your dreams of London.

South Kensington. Diana lived there.

Knightsbridge. That's where Harrods is.

Hyde Park Corner. That's where you can scream crazy ideas at anyone who will listen.

Green Park. That's by Buckingham Palace, where the Queen lives.

Piccadilly Circus. That's where the famous billboards are.

Leicester Square. That's where the theaters and cinemas are.

Covent Garden. That's where the famous market is.

Holborn. You don't know what's there. You can't place it.

Then, you get to Russell Square. It's your stop!

Stand up!

Wake up!

You're in London!

The train comes to a stop. You push your way out with your bags and everyone makes way – just another tourist arriving in London.

You step out onto the platform, a beautiful circular space, with green tiling all around. An old clock hangs above the platform. There are giant ads opposite the platform, adverting things Londoners should be interested in or buying. You see one for the movie you hoped to see while in London; it won't open back home for months. You stand for a brief second, searching for the black and yellow "Way Out" sign. As you begin your walk along the platform, the train accelerates out of the station, and it makes the most wonderful sound.

It takes a gush of wind with it and fills your nose with the smell of London's grime, cleaners, and detritus. It's the most wonderful smell, not like that urine and cigarette smell you get on the Paris Metro. You've arrived in London. You follow the signs to the exit and arrive at the lift. It feels like it takes ages to get there, then ages to get you to the surface. You wonder just how far underground you are.

The elevator deposits you into the ticket hall and the gate line ahead of you. It's the most wonderfully old space, almost exactly as it was over a hundred years ago when it was opened for the first time. As you tap your Oyster card (because you're a tourist who comes prepared) and exit the station, you turn around and admire the beautiful crimson station tiles. This has to be one of the most beautifully designed stations on the network.

You turn right thinking that's the way to your hotel, but as you go a few blocks and check your map again, you realize it was left, so you immediately turn around and head back towards the station, passing it again.

You enter Russell Square, a beautiful leafy green space in the middle of the city, and soon find your hotel. As you suspected, it's too early to check in, but you're able to leave your bags with the concierge. You leave the hotel and find a café; time for a quick breakfast and a cup of tea to get you going. You find a hole in the wall, a place where local workers gather - not the kind of place tourists swamp. The food is hearty, greasy, and delicious. The two cups of tea you down wake you up and prepare you to make the most of your first day in London.

You get up and walk back to the Tube station, tap in, and go down to the platforms - this time awake and aware of where you are.

You're in London properly. Finally!

You look at the map between the platforms; you're not sure where you want to go. There are so many possibilities — so many favorites. You immediately think, "All right, if I go to Covent Garden, I can get a Ben's cookie, then see the market, then walk down Long Acre towards Trafalgar Square to see some art at the National Gallery." Already, that's the perfect start to any trip to London.

You turn right towards the platform. It's relatively empty now. It's late morning. Londoners are at work. The Tube is now for the tourists, and you can take it anywhere in London. It's now *your* London. The dot matrix sign above the platform indicates there's a train approaching in two minutes. You wonder how accurate that it is. When the train arrives in two minutes, you realize it's very accurate. You hop on the train.

"Please mind the gap," the voice tells you again.

And you're off. Next Stop Covent Garden. Next stop your London trip you've waited so long for, your London dream.

Your trip to London has finally begun properly. No more airports, no more shuffling. The Tube will take you everywhere you want to go now. It will hold you, it will keep you safe, and it will transport you. When you leave London a few days later, you'll miss it. You'll miss that rocking feeling and holding the railings for dear life. You'll miss the free newspapers in the late afternoon, handed out at each station. You'll miss the smells as the Tube comes into the station and you're hit with that gust of wind. You'll miss watching the platform, hoping to see the station mice scurry about. You'll miss watching the darkness of the tunnel ahead in anticipation of the lights announcing the arrival of your train. Most of all, you'll miss the sense of exploration. You'll miss stepping onto a platform, open to the possibility of traveling anywhere on the almost 400-station network. London is all yours to see and explore.

Most of all, you'll miss just being there and inhabiting the place.

"Please mind the gap."

You wonder if you can bottle the sounds, the smells, and the feelings to take home with you.

You can't.

But you always have a reason to come back, again and again.

BOOKS ABOUT THE TUBE

The Tube is one of the most written-about aspects of London's History. I have several shelves full of books about the London Tube. Here are a few of my favorites:

London's Underground: The Story of the Tube by Oliver Green - In this major work published in association with Transport for London, Tube expert Oliver Green traces the history of the Underground, following its troubles and triumphs, its wartime and peacetime work, and the essential part it has played in shaping London's economy, geography, tourism and identity. Specially commissioned photography by Benjamin Graham (UK Landscape Photographer of the Year 2017) brings the story to life in vivid portraits of London Underground's stations, tunnels and trains.

Hidden London: Discovering the Forgotten Underground - Hidden London is a lavishly illustrated history of disused and repurposed London Underground spaces. It provides the first narrative of a previously secret and barely understood aspect of London's history. Behind locked doors and lost entrances lies a secret world of abandoned stations, redundant passageways, empty elevator shafts, and cavernous ventilation ducts. The Tube is an ever-expanding network that has left in its wake hidden places and spaces. Hidden London opens up the lost worlds of London's Underground and offers a fascinating analysis of why Underground spaces—including the deep-level shelter at Clapham South, the closed Aldwych station, the lost tunnels of Euston—have fallen into disuse and how they have been repurposed. With access to previously unseen archives, architectural drawings, and images, the authors create an authoritative account of London's hidden Underground story. This surprising and at times myth-breaking narrative interweaves spectacular, newly commissioned photography of disused stations and Underground structures today.

London Underground By Design - London Underground By Design is the beautifully illustrated new book from Mark Ovenden, the acclaimed author of Great Railway Maps of the World, published to coincide with the 150th anniversary of the Tube in 2013.

The Tube Mapper Project: Capturing Moments on the London Underground Hardcover – by Luke Agbaimon - The Underground is the backbone of the city of London, a part of our identity. It's a network of shared experiences and visual memories. The Tube Mapper project deliberately captures moments of subconscious recognition and overlooked interests, showcasing images that can be seen near or at every Underground, Overground and DLR station in London. Photographer Luke Agbaimoni gave up city-scape night photography after the birth of his first child, but creating Tube Mapper allowed him to continue being creative, fitting photography around his new lifestyle, and adding stations on his daily commute. His memorable photographs include themes of symmetry, reflections, tunnels and escalators, waiting and lines of light, and reveals the London every commuter knows in a unique, vibrant and arresting style.

London Under: The Secret History Beneath the Streets Paperback – by Peter Ackroyd - In this vividly descriptive short study, Peter Ackroyd tunnels down through the geological layers of London, meeting the creatures that dwell in darkness and excavating the lore and mythology beneath the surface.

Walk the Lines: The London Underground, Overground by Mark Mason - As a lifelong fan of London, Mark Mason embarks on a mission to 'conquer' the capital once and for all. The only way to truly discover a city, they say, is on foot. Taking this to extremes, Mark sets out to walk the entire length of the London Underground - overground - passing every station on the way. Over the course of several hundred miles, he comes to understand a sprawling metropolis that never ceases to surprise.

BEST TUBE PHONE APPS

There are several apps to help you make the best use of the London Underground. Some are officials from Transport for London; some are put out by third parties. Here's a rundown of the best ones. All are available on iOS or Android.

TFL Go - A very simple and slick app put out by Transport for London. It has the whole Tube map and a journey planner. It will also help you use alternative forms of transport - like buses.

Tube Map - London Underground - An unofficial Tube app, but it's also very good. It has a Tube map along with a handy journey planner. It has a little bit more information when you plan your route and can help you reroute if you need to.

TFL Oyster - This app will let you manage your Oyster Card and top it up without having to do it at the station. It doesn't work with older cards.

Citymapper - This is the Ulitmate London transport app, and it's completely free. It won't just help you plan your route; it'll help you get to where you want to go from the station. It will also help you book a taxi if you like.

Station Master - The Ultimate Tube Nerd app, this app will help you navigate the Tube, but also navigate it smartly - like telling you which train car to get in that's closest to the exit at your destination station. There's trivia about each station and cool 3D maps.

TUBE YOUTUBERS

Transport YouTube is one of the most popular subjects on the video streaming website. There are several notable Tube YouTubers, who cover the London Underground, some in excruciating but fascinating detail. Just search for these names on YouTube and you'll find them.

Geoff Marshall - Basically the God of all things London Transport, he releases several videos a week about the Tube and trains around London (as well as the rest of Britain).

Jay Foreman - Makes great videos about the history and culture of London, not exclusively about the Tube but has many videos about the Tube. His videos are usually very funny and informative.

Jago Hazzard - A channel very loosely focused on London, trains, history, and combinations thereof. The home of Tales from the Tube, Jago's Trains, Streets of London, and Useful Beer Reviews.

RM Transit - He covered city-based transit systems around the world but has quite a few videos about London's transport system.

Hidden London Hangouts - These started during the pandemic, but they've continued beyond. A group of employees at the London Transport Museum publishes regular videos about meetups, and they explore interesting parts of the Tube network.

Tim Dunn - The host of TV shows about trains, also regularly posts videos to YouTube about the Tube and other neat train stuff.

Ruairidh MacVeigh - Another YouTuber that makes videos about British transport history but also covers the Tube regularly.

USING THE TUBE

1 Cockfosters
No Smoking
2 mins
09:28:45
KNIGHTSBRIDGE

TOP 10 ETIQUETTE TIPS FOR THE TOURIST ON THE LONDON UNDERGROUND

We thought it would be useful to put together some etiquette tips for riding the Tube so that you don't make a pillock of yourself on the Tube.

1. NO TALKING

Never talk to anyone other than in your own party and even that will be frowned upon if you must, do so quietly. The Tube is not really a place to try to pick up a lady. People live in their own personal bubbles when they ride the Tube, and Londoners prefer it that way. Many like to read, so don't disturb their quality reading time.

2. GIVE UP YOUR SEAT FOR AN OLD OR PREGNANT WOMAN

If you see a pregnant woman or a woman wearing a 'I'm Pregnant' pin, do the honorable thing and give them your seat. This was

a lifesaver for my wife when she traveled the underground network while she was pregnant. The same goes for an elderly or disabled person.
Hell, even if you want to be a gentleman, give up your seat for any lady (even if she's not attractive).
Just don't try to talk to her after you do.

3. THOUGH IT IS QUITE TEMPTING, DON'T READ OVER OTHER PEOPLE'S SHOULDERS

One of my favorite things about traveling on the Tube is you get an idea of what's popular reading with Londoners. That said, don't be tempted to read over anyone's shoulders – people can feel your eyes on their stuff, and it will make them uncomfortable. It's especially tempting if they're reading the newspapers (most especially Page 3 of the Sun).

4. LET PASSENGERS OFF THE TRAIN BEFORE TRYING TO GET ON

I know you're excited to get on the Tube – but please let people get off first before you try to get on. You won't miss the train, and if you do – there will be another one in a few minutes. This gets a little tricky when the train is really busy but try to keep in mind that everyone is trying to get where they're going. A little courtesy goes a long way.

5. YOUR BAG OR SUITCASE IS NOT ENTITLED TO A SEAT, ESPECIALLY IF THE TRAIN IS CROWDED

This is a biggie. In Chicago (where Londontopia.net is based), it's pretty common to avoid getting too close to your fellow passenger by using your bag as a seat partner deterrent. Do not do this on the Tube. The Tube is overcrowded, and most people have to stand, so if you take up a seat with yourself and another seat with your bag – expect steely stares. If you insist on riding the Tube during rush hour with all your luggage – stick to the back of the cabin where there's room for luggage.

6. WATCH OUT FOR PICKPOCKETS

Pickpockets are everywhere in London, but they particularly love Tube stations because they're loud and noisy, and it's easy to pick pockets in all the confusion. Keep your valuables in difficult-to-access places (for thieves, that is).

7. STAND ON THE RIGHT ON THE ESCALATORS

You'll be reminded of this on every escalator, but it bears repeating here – always stand on the right on the escalators. People who are in a bigger hurry than you will speed past you on the left. Best not to get in the way. If you do – you may get a courteous "Scuse me Love" or a not-so-courteous "get out of the way."

8. WEAR DEODORANT OR COLOGNE. PLEASE.

The Tube is hot and crowded in the summer. The network is 150 years old and was not designed for air conditioning. It gets hot in the fall and the spring too. No one wants to stand in a crowded Tube car or platform near someone who smells. So, wear some odor protection. But don't overdo it!

9. HAVE YOUR OYSTER CARD OR TICKET READY

The novelty of going through a Tube station can be confusing to new travelers in London. That confusion causes much delays for fellow passengers. Always have your ticket or Oyster Card ready when going through the ticket gates. That includes going in the station and out of the station. You have to have a valid ticket to get out – so never throw your ticket away and always have it ready.

10. DON'T EAT ON THE TRAIN

When surveyed about annoying Tube Habits, Londoners said this was the one that bothered them the most: eating smelling food anywhere on the network. Your lunch or dinner is not a shared experience, so avoid turning anyone's stomach by not eating anywhere on the network unless it's in a train station in a restaurant.

HOW TO GET AN OYSTER CARD

An Oyster Card is an electronic card used across the Tube network, on buses, trams, DLR, London Overground, TfL Rail, River Bus and most National Rail services in London. See the Transport for London website tfl.gov.uk for full details. Note that London buses are now all cashless, so you need to use an Oyster card, Travelcard or contactless payment.

You swipe your Oyster card to get through the gates at any Tube station, and tap it when getting on a bus or tram. It's a much quicker way to travel across the network than using tickets, and it's very popular.

It's popular because you always get the lowest fare possible when you use it. If you use the Tube or bus several times during the day, you won't pay more than a certain price for your entire day of journeys. Use of the Oyster card is also heavily discounted – you save over 50% versus paying cash for a ticket.

Before you leave for London, buy a Visitor Oyster card. It's much cheaper than buying a day or week pass. You can purchase them easily from the Visit Britain website, or you can also buy one in London, but it's easier to do so before you get there. They're pretty much good forever, I've had mine for over a decade and just refill it when I'm in London.

London's transport system also supports contactless credit cards (the kind you can hover or tap,) and you can access the network with just one of those, bypassing the need for an Oyster Card. Your usage will still be tracked, and at the end of the day you'll be charged the lowest fare for all your use.

We should note that most tickets offices on the Tube are now closed, so you have to either have an Oyster Card already, use a contactless card, or purchase a ticket from a vending machine (this is the most expensive option).

LONDON TRANSPORT OPERATING HOURS

This is the biggest change to the Tube in recent years is that there is now a Night Tube 24 hour service on some Tube lines. The rest of the Tube closes after midnight and opens around 5 am depending on the line.

Night Tube is currently running on Friday and Saturday nights on the Central, Jubilee, Northern, Piccadilly and Victoria lines. This was at the time of publication in Autumn 2022, this will likely change as the pandemic changed the way the Tube operates in so many ways.

Don't fret! If you miss the last Tube train, you have options!

If you plan to be out late, and you don't have a Night Tube line, you'll need to rely on London Black Taxis or the bus to get back to your hotel.

The bus system runs 24 hours, so you can always rely on that to get where you need to go. Buses are also cheaper than the Tube, and you'll get more local color this way.

You can expect London Black Taxis to operate through the night, but they will become harder to find them the later (and earlier) it gets. Avoid minicabs at all costs as they are unlicensed and don't require the training that Black Cab drivers have. We've also had strange experiences when looking for a cab where random people will offer us a ride. Don't ever do this.

Uber and other ride-sharing apps have completely changed this; you can now hire a cab from your phone pretty much anywhere safely.

WHAT MAKES THE ELIZABETH LINE DIFFERENT FROM OTHER UNDERGROUND LINES?

If you've looked at the London Underground map lately, you may have noticed a sharp purple line cutting from east to west. This is the new Elizabeth Line, formerly known as Crossrail, a hybrid commuter rail and rapid transit service. It has been in development since 2005 and finally opened this year after financial and construction setbacks caused in part by the COVID-19 pandemic. Now in service alongside the London Underground, it has several notable differences that set it apart from the Tube, from the trains themselves to the line's operation. First and foremost, it is not a 'tube line' - it is a regular national railway line. But it coexists and operates side-by-side with the London Underground.

Perhaps the biggest and most obvious difference are the trains themselves. While the London Underground lines stock are either S7 or S8, the Elizabeth Line uses Class 345 trains. The Elizabeth Line's 345 stock are based on the Aventa similar, but improved, to that used by other British Rail trains. The 345 is more suited to sub-surface passenger carrying but more powerful and faster than the average S7/S8. To give you an idea of the difference, the top speed of the Underground stock is about 62 mph while the 345 can do 90 mph. The 345 was made exclusively for Crossrail and is truly a hybrid between the Underground trains and the British Rail stock. Class 345 trains can also transport up to 1500 passengers per train.

The management of the two commuter systems is also different. While Transport for London has exclusive management of the London Underground, the Elizabeth Line is part-owned by TfL, National Rail, and Heathrow Airport Holdings. A separate management firm named MTR Corporation was granted an eight-year contract to operate Crossrail. Originating in Hong Kong in 1972, MTR manages mass transit systems throughout the world, including China, Australia, and Sweden. Additionally, unlike the rest of the London Underground, the Elizabeth Line presently only operates Monday through Saturday and has no service on Sundays (this will change).

When it comes to the Elizabeth Line's support, it sets itself apart from the London Underground yet again. This Crossrail line has its own depot at Old Oak Common in West London and can service 42 of the line's 70 trains at any given time. The Elizabeth Line also has a total of 41 stations with their own unique design, as the white curves of the platform tunnels feel like walking through the bones of some gigantic creature. The new stations for the line have their own modernist feel when coming out of the tunnels with glistening metal paneling that would make a good set for another Star Wars film (much as Canary Wharf did for Rogue One).

One of the largest changes is one that most of us probably wouldn't recognize. For those passengers with mobility issues, they'll be pleased to know that, unlike the rest of the London Underground, the Elizabeth Line is fully accessible. From street to platform, each station is step free, making it easier for all passengers to make their way to the train and onboard for their journey across London. And once inside, you'll notice the trains have their own unique Moquette pattern in the line's distinctive purple Pantone 275. Lastly, one thing that's very important to point out and a bit of a detriment for the line is that the Oyster card won't work for the entirety of the Elizabeth Line. Once you get past West Drayton, Oyster cannot be used, and passengers either need to use contactless or purchase a paper ticket for further travel. Most tourists, however, will only be using Oyster on the Elizabeth line in Central London but be warned if you venture further out.

So, as you can see, while the Elizabeth Line might be a bright new addition to the London Underground map, it is both part of and separate from the rest of the Tube. From the trains to the stations to how you use it, it has many distinct qualities that set it apart. Keep these in mind before you use the Elizabeth Line service, and we hope you have a wonderful journey.

TEN OF THE BEST-LOOKING TUBE STATIONS TO VISIT

In cities throughout the world, we use public transportation every day, but we don't often look around at the subway, bus, and train stations as we pass through them. If we did, we might find some very attractive public spaces that are worth more than a quick glance. London, over the years, has attempted to make its Underground Stations into works of art, be it the original Victorian design stations or newer stops such as Canary Wharf. We've outlined ten of the most attractive Tube stations for you to visit on your next trip to London and marvel at their brilliance.

GLOUCESTER RD

On the outside, the Gloucester Rd Tube Station is already a work of art thanks to the classic red-tilled design of architect Leslie Green. Inside the station was nothing remarkable until its disused eastbound station was turned into a temporary art gallery in 2000. The space is now so popular that it's often used for special events.

WESTMINSTER

Brutalism can get a pretty bad rap as an architectural style considering its just geometrical concrete, but sometimes it can produce some really lovely designs, such as the Westminster Underground Station. The mix of stone columns and metal pipes creates a clean, industrial look that contrasts with intricately designed buildings above, but yet still feels like it fits in.

CANARY WHARF

Perhaps one of the most postmodern-looking Underground Stations on this list, Canary Wharf appears so futuristic that it was actually used as a movie set in the Star Wars movie Rogue One as an Imperial base (albeit with some dressing up). The escalators at the entrance are worthy enough on their own, but once you get down into the bowels of the station, you'll find the subsurface architecture just as fascinating.

GANTS HILL

In the 1930s, architect Charles Holden was inspired by the Moscow Metro in the creation of the Gants Hill Underground Station. The concourse actually has no above-surface buildings and uses pedestrian walkways to take you to the ticket station and then escalators down to the barrel-vaulted train platforms.

EARL'S COURT

Earl's Court is another tube station bathed in natural light thanks to a steel-framed skylight. The Underground platforms themselves have that classic white tiling you'll see throughout older Tube stations. The outside is also notable for being home to London's only remaining Police Public Call Box, though don't knock on the outside expecting the Doctor to open the door.

KINGS CROSS ST. PANCRAS

Kings Cross St. Pancras is one of the most important stations not only in London, but all over the United Kingdom since it serves both the London Underground and National Rail. As such, the station's design is suitably impressive, combining the original Victorian architecture with more modern designs, evident by both the large vaulted steel skylight on the train platforms of St. Pancras and the King's Cross Station entrance.

BAKER STREET

The baker Street Underground Station is definitely the place for Sherlock Holmes fans. Not only is it close to the Sherlock Holmes Museum that's set up as a recreation of his fictional 221B Baker Street flat, but the Tube station walls are lined with tiles that feature his silhouette with iconic pipe and deerstalker cap. The arching brick roof on the train platform is also pretty beautiful and doesn't exist in many other places in the Underground.

TOTTENHAM COURT ROAD

The Tottenham Court Road station is an interesting mixture of the old and the new. In the 1980s, Scottish artist Eduardo Paolozzi designed over 1,000 square meters of tiled mosaics throughout the station. When the station was expanded for Crossrail, some of the mosaics were taken out and replaced with clean white tiles, though 95% of Paolozzi's mosaics still remain in the station. Don't worry, though, as the other 5% were restored and toured the UK as an art exhibit.

LEYTONSTONE

And while we're on the subject of tiled mosaics, you can find some pretty gorgeous ones that pay homage to one of the area's most famous residents. In 1999, seventeen mosaics went up throughout the station dedicated to director Alfred Hitchcock. Created one hundred years after Hitchcock's birth, they feature important scenes from many of his movies from The Birds to North by Northwest.

SOUTHWARK

Southwark Tube Station's design is akin to a dystopian future movie with stark shite stone, gleaming metal, and bold shapes throughout. No matter what level you're on, it feels like you're in a different time and place whenever you travel through the station. Fritz Lang would probably feel right at home here if he was still around.

WAY OUT

TOP TUBE USAGE SECRET TIPS

Rather than expand these into their own chapters, here's our list of handy Tube Tips for making the best use of London's Underground. These tips, learned from twenty years of travel in London, will turn you into a Tube pro in no time!

1. Don't Use Covent Garden - This station is too small for the amount of people that use it - so don't. Use Leicester Square down the street; it's literally a few hundred feet away. You're going to walk the same distance anyway.

2. Forget your Oyster Card? They're no longer needed; you can tap in and out of the Tube with any Contactless credit card, and you will be charged the same rate you would for an Oyster Card

3. Get a Tube App - Get the official Tube App - it will help you plan your journey and give you a Tube map to guide you along the network.

4. There's WiFi and Cell Service Now - There is WiFi network-

wide on the Tube now, and there are now several cell networks also working through the Tubes. Don't count on it, though.

5. Stand on the right - Always stand on the right on escalators so people can get by you if they're in a hurry.

6. Mind the Gap - Be careful of the gap between the platforms and the actual trains, it's a trip hazard, and you can get seriously hurt.

7. Avoid Changing at Bank - You may end up walking through seemingly miles of tunnels; as you connect between lines, they're farther apart than you think. It might be better to walk on the surface streets!

8. For Trafalgar Square, use Charing Cross.

9. To get a great view of the Palace of Westminster, take the Tube to Waterloo and then walk along the Thames path to Westminster Bridge; you can see the whole lovely Palace and Big Ben (bonus book market under Waterloo Bridge along the way).

10. There is no longer any open tickets office at Tube Stations; you have to use the automated machines (though with contactless - see above - you don't need to buy a 'ticket'). There will be staff wandering around to help you if you're confused.

11. The Tube is only just starting to operate for 24 hours, and even then, only on select lines and routes. Double-check the opening/closing times for your journey to make sure you're not caught out without a train. Otherwise, it's the night bus for you (like in Harry Potter).

12. Most Tube stations won't have a bathroom, but the mainline railway stations that the Tube shares will usually have public bathrooms (now most are unpaid).

13. The entire network is not step-free, so wheelchair access

depends on the station and the route. Check the Tube Map, as it will tell you which stations are step-free. The new Elizabeth Line is completely step-free.

14. The Piccadilly Line is the cheapest way to get from Heathrow to Central London. It's rather slow, though. However, you can now take the Elizabeth directly from Heathrow to Central London, but it costs exactly double the price. It's much faster, though!

15. You cannot take the Tube to Gatwick Airport, but you can take the Gatwick Express (or National Rail, which is usually cheaper).

16. There are several abandoned Tube stations along the network for various reasons. There are regular tours offered through the London Transport Museum called the Hidden London Tours, which take in these special stations. They are very much worth doing.

17. Watch out for women wearing the baby on board button; its proper tube Etiquette to give up your seat for them (or the elderly, for that matter).

18. The open door button is a lie. The doors are going to open automatically. You never need to press it. Though pressing it provides some kind of impatient relief.

19. The Tube gets very hot in the summer months - for several reasons. While some newer trains and lines may be air-conditioned, most still aren't, and neither are the stations. It's going to be hot and sweaty underground. Drink plenty of water and be prepared to get hot.

20. Weekend trains aren't nearly as frequent as peak weekday trains, so be prepared to wait for the next train (and the dot matrix display will always tell you when to expect the next train).

21. Avoid Rush Hours - This is when the Tube is the busiest as people are trying to get to and from work. Avoid the Tube at

these times: (7.30 am–9.30 am and 5.00 pm–7.00 pm). Locals will thank you, especially if you have luggage.

22. Don't try to bring a bike on the Tube; you're not allowed on many of the Tube lines. And certainly don't bring a 'Boris Bike' on the Tube either.

23. Luggage - Try to avoid using the Tube with a ton of luggage, especially at Rush Hour. There's simply no room on the trains for luggage.

24. Let people off the train first before trying to get on.

25. Keep personal belongings close to you and keep credit cards and valuables in a place hard for a pickpocket to get to.

GETTING AROUND LONDON
A BRIEF PRIMER ON PUBLIC TRANSPORT IN LONDON

In a city as large as London, public transport is a must for getting from place to place. Starting in the 19th Century, public transport became a necessity as more people began moving to the suburbs. The first horse-drawn omnibuses began in 1829, the North London Railway in 1850, and the Metropolitan Railway in 1853 (the predecessor for the Underground), though the first hackney carriages came about as early as 1654.

Each of these has a modern equivalent to help Londoners and tourists get around. These services as managed by Transport for London, the local governmental body responsible for public transportation across London. However, the first thing you need to know is that most forms of public transport require an Oyster Card.

Oyster Cards are an electronic form of ticketing issued by TfL that covers the London Underground, trams, certain riverboat services, London buses, light rail, and some National Railway services operating within London. There are some limitations, however, since some National Railway services are not under the control of TfL and private companies can refuse to honor the card.

Perhaps the best and most well-known public transport system in London is the London Underground. With 270 stations and 11 lines servicing the city, it's one of the easiest and most convenient ways to get around, especially if you're already familiar with other subways systems. One drawback to the Underground is six of London's thirty-two boroughs are not serviced by the Underground, including: Bexley, Bromley, Croydon, Kingston, Lewisham, and Sutton. Peak service times can also slow down your wait to get from station to station, making it so that walking the distance ends up being faster. Still, it's a classic way to move through London.

Like most cities large and small, the city operates its own bus service. London Buses even operate in boroughs where you can't find a London Underground station. Besides just the Oyster Card, the buses accept Travelcards, debit, and credit cards. Since July of this year, however, they don't accept cash anymore. Additionally, another great reason to ride London Buses is their iconic status. London Buses represented some of the first double-decker buses in the world and the Routemaster is the most recognized. If you're lucky, you might even get to ride its newest incarnation, the New Routemaster, also known as Borisbuses or the Borismaster after Boris Johnson, the Mayor of London.

Another option for boroughs without the London Underground is Tramlink, an overground light rail system that serves South London. The Docklands Light Railway operates in East and Southeast London. Local trains are also an option, including the London Overground, Silverlink, SouthEastern Railway, Southern Railway, and East Anglia lines.

One form of transport being embraced by cities, including London, is a bike-share program. The London Cycle Hire Scheme isn't a scam, but a chance to rent a bicycle from several stations around the city. What's best is that you never have to worry about service delays or mechanical breakdowns. Just check out a bike at one station (first half-hour is free) and return it at another. Also called "Boris bikes," it's a great transport system and form of exercise.

Feel like a nice day on the River Thames? Thames River Buses are a commuter service with routes up and down the river, plus some of the River Buses even come with Wi-Fi and refreshments. All in all, there are about six different routes and stops that include the London Bridge, the Tower of London, the Tate Modern, Tate Britain, and the O2. Several river cruises are also available for those that want more of a touristy trip on the Thames.

Last, but certainly not least, are the famous London Black Cabs. A Black Cab is one of the quickest, most direct ways to get where you're going. To even drive one of these coveted transports, cabbies have to pass a test of London streets called "The Knowledge". Minicabs are also an option, but run the risk of being unlicensed, unsafe, and illegal. Black Cabs are the safest taxi service around the city, and London even offers the Cabwise app to book licensed and regulated minicabs. Additionally, texting CAB to the number 60835 will give you the number for two licensed minicabs and one Black Cab.

Acknowledgements

While many different writing voices combined to make this book possible, we must single out longtime Anglotopia/Londontopia contributor John Rabon, who wrote many of the original articles that were adapted into this book. His tireless research on all things related to the Tube turned out to be a great foundation for this book. Thank you for all your hard work, John!

About Anglotopia.net

Anglotopia.net is the world's largest website for people who love Britain. Founded in 2007, it has grown to be the biggest community of passionate Anglophiles anywhere. With daily updates covering British Culture, History, and Travel - Anglotopia is the place to get your British Fix!

https://anglotopia.net
https://londontopia.net